OTHER BOOKS BY DR. BILLY GRAHAM

Approaching Hoofbeats
How to Be Born Again
The Holy Spirit
Till Armageddon
Peace with God
The Secret of Happiness
Angels: God's Secret Agents
Unto the Hills

FACING
DEATH
AND THE
LIFE AFTER

Billy Graham

FACING DEATH

AND THE LIFE AFTER

Grason
Minneapolis, MN

FACING DEATH—AND THE LIFE AFTER

Copyright © 1987 by Billy Graham

Unless otherwise indicated, Scripture quotations are from the New International Version of the Bible, published by the Zondervan Corporation, copyright © 1973 by the New York Bible Society. Used by permission.

Those marked NASB are from the New American Standard Bible, copyright © 1960, 1962, 1963, 1968, 1971 by the Lockman Foundation.

Those marked KJV are from the King James Version.

Those marked LB are from the Living Bible, © 1971 Tyndale House Publishers, used by permission.

Excerpt from "Lament" by Edna St. Vincent Millay. From *Collected Poems*, Harper & Row. Copyright © 1921, 1948 by Edna St. Vincent Millay. Reprinted by permission.

Library of Congress Cataloging-in-Publication Data

Graham, Billy, 1918–
    Facing death and the life after.

    1. Death—Religious aspects—Christianity.
2. Future life—Christianity.   I. Title.
BT825.G64   1987   236'.1   87–15930
ISBN 0–8499–0474–9

Printed in the United States of America

7898 RRD 987654

Then I heard a voice from heaven say,
"Write: Blessed are the dead who die in the
Lord from now on."
  "Yes," says the Spirit, "they will rest
from their labor, for their deeds will follow them."

Revelation 14:13

CONTENTS

INTRODUCTION

Man is destined to die once, and after that to face judgment.

Hebrews 9:27

The 563 men, women and children who boarded *The Herald of Free Enterprise* ferry on March 6, 1987, in Zeebrugge, Belgium, for a trip across the English Channel to Dover, England, had no inkling of what awaited them shortly after leaving the harbor.

Without warning, the four-thousand-ton vessel began to list and within seconds, the happy passengers were transformed into desperate, terrified people as they plunged beneath the icy cold waters and began to battle for their lives.

Two hundred passengers and crew members went to a watery grave. The only reason the toll was not much higher was the quick work by rescue crews who risked their own lives to save others.

More recently, thirty-seven men lost their lives on the USS *Stark* in the Persian Gulf, and some twenty-nine people died when a tornado struck the little town of Saragosa in West Texas. We have grown used to hearing about (and even seeing) such tragedies reported on our television newscasts and tend to treat them as mere statistics unless one of our loved ones is involved.

It is an axiom that there are just two certainties in life: death and taxes, but that is not true. With the right deductions and a good accountant, millionaires have managed to avoid paying any taxes at all. But everyone, millionaires and paupers, will face the ultimate certainty: death.

It is doubtful that any of the passengers aboard the ferry thought about the possibility of their being dead within minutes after boarding the vessel. That is largely because we live in a death-denying society.

Even the language and atmosphere of funeral homes denies death. A person who has died is said to have "departed." The person is stripped of his or her name and referred to as a "loved one." There are persons who are specialists in applying makeup to a dead body to make it appear as if the person is only sleeping.

Advertisers do all they can to help us deny the ultimate fact of life. Billions of dollars are spent on a cosmetic industry that promises creams and lotions will slow the aging process and make the user look younger. Joggers line the roads, often before dawn, and workouts at health clubs have become popular ways to keep the body in shape to prolong life. Fiber is an increasingly prevalent part of some people's diets as physicians tell us of its ability to reduce the risk of cancer. Many people are giving up smoking to reduce the possibility of heart and lung disease.

But the irreversible fact is that no matter what your

10

diet, no matter how much you exercise, no matter how many vitamins or health foods you eat, no matter how low your cholesterol, you will still die—someday, some way. You may add a year, or even a few years to a life that could be shorter had you not been concerned about your health, but in the end death will conquer you as it has every person who has ever lived.

If you knew the moment and manner of your death in advance, would you order your life differently? If so, when would you do it . . . right now, or would you wait until the day before? And then what would you do to right the mistakes you made during your life?

Unfortunately, no one knows the day or the hour of his death, which is why it is best, in the words of the scout motto, to "be prepared."

It is my prayer that this book may be a source of support and blessing for every reader, and that each of us will have the comfort of God's love as we face the issues discussed here. For those who do not know Christ, I pray they will meet Him in these pages.

Naturally, I have not written this book alone. Others have helped immensely. Especially do I owe a deep debt of gratitude to my longtime friend Carole Carlson. She did so much research for the first of many drafts of the manuscript. Without her, this book would have been almost impossible to finish on time. Then, as always, I want to thank my wife, Ruth, for her part in helping to plan and shape this book and for sharing a number of touching moments from her own life. For years, she has kept a file of material on the subject of death (as she does on many subjects, to help me in my preaching and writing). Some of the stories and statistics in this book came from her files. I also want to thank Dr. John Akers, the Reverend

Jack Black, Mrs. Millie Dienert, and Dr. Harold Lindsell who read and made helpful comments and additions to sections of the book.

Further, I want to thank each of the other men and women who have supported me in researching and developing this work and in preparing it for publication. Likewise, a word of appreciation to my publisher, Ernie Owen, and my editors, Al Bryant and Dr. Jim Black of Word. And, last but not least, a special thank you to my secretary, Stephanie Wills, for her tireless effort and unflagging support.

1

THE LAST ENEMY

"If we are in a battle with this enemy called Death, I believe we should learn about it, in order to know how to confront the dying experience. We need to know how to face that enemy on our own behalf, and how to deal with the inevitable deaths of loved ones and friends."

The last enemy that will be abolished is death.

1 Corinthians 15:26 NASB

A twisted pile of metal and shattered glass lay like a broken toy in the left lane of the freeway. The flares, police cars, ambulances, and flashing red lights created a scene of sudden and ominous dread. An expensive sports car, once an object of pride, now lay twisted beyond repair. A limp body sprawled in the front seat, wedged beneath the steering wheel. Was the victim alive or dead? Could the mangled body be stitched together by the hands of a skilled surgeon, or would it be hastily covered with a plastic sheet and transported unceremoniously to the city morgue, "DOA, dead on arrival"?

For all of the shock and anguish for the loved ones and families affected by such tragedies, scenes like this one are repeated every day on America's highways. The grief we feel at the sudden death of a loved one can be crushing; yet, such accidents are all too common. Only spectacular disasters make the headlines any more, and families whose lives have been suddenly shattered and their futures dramatically changed, discover too late that they are unprepared.

What about that anonymous driver? Was he prepared for the sudden change in his future plans? Had he arranged his affairs for such a possibility, and had he considered his options for eternity?

How we deal with death and tragedy says a lot about what kind of people we are. All too often we glance at the newspaper and notice that another celebrity has died; a phone call or letter brings sad news about a friend's death. We hurt for our loved ones and mourn our own losses, but how prepared are we to face death as a reality and deal with the difficult challenges it creates?

I remember an incident in Paris in September of 1986, just before the beginning of our crusade. We were having a fairly normal day of business when, suddenly, it seemed like this beautiful city was under siege. A bomb exploded in a busy department store during the noon rush hour, killing and wounding women and children. We discovered we had arrived during a series of terrorist attacks, an onslaught which *Time* magazine decried, calling the new wave of terrorism "this leprosy of modern times."[1]

As it turned out, we were never seriously threatened by that wave of sudden violence, and I have my own feelings about why that might be, but, nevertheless, we had to think about the dire possibilities and what consequences our crusade team might have to anticipate. By nature, the human mind does not want to deal with distasteful facts. We want to forget the unpleasant or painful and concentrate on the "positive." We persuade ourselves that sudden death happens to others, not to us. But that is not always so.

Death: The Final Certainty

Death tolls in wars and epidemics, and the news we read of famine in foreign lands, draw our attention to the fatal aspects of the world around us. Reports from Africa and South America tell of millions of affected citizens, thousands of casualties, miles of affected territory, months and years of suffering, and all the tragedy that can be summed up in statistical fashion. But statistics, and the ways they are fed to us by the media, can be misleading. Death is perennial. During World War II, C. S. Lewis pointed out that war does not increase death; death is total in every generation. It takes every one of us. George Bernard Shaw wryly wrote, "The statistics on death are quite impressive. One out of one people die."

During family week at a Christian conference center, a message came that one of the couples who had been teachers for many of the children at the camp had walked into their four-month-old baby's room and found him blue and lifeless—a victim of crib death. A pall came over everyone as the news spread. Why did this happen to people like Ben and Sally? She was in her late thirties and this was their first child. She taught her kindergarten class until shortly before her baby was due, and every day her little pupils prayed for that baby. Ben and Sally's students and members of their church were excited when little Benjamin was born. Why did the Lord take him?

Death is so often accompanied by those heartbreaking questions, "Why me? Why now? Why this?"

Why must we die? The Bible says, "It is appointed unto men once to die" (Hebrews 9:27 KJV). It is the most democratic of all experiences. Over 400 years ago the English author John Heywood noted, "Death makes equal the high and low." We can fight it, and the will to fight it is instinctive. We can even avoid it for a time, and common sense allows us that privilege. We can argue, plead, and bargain, but death is the one universal enemy. Saying "I don't want to think about it" won't make the reality disappear. Death ultimately intrudes into our well-planned lives and changes things around, absolutely.

We want to deny death. We cover our awkwardness around the subject by speaking of the deceased as if they did not die. "He departed this life," we say. "He passed away," or "He's gone up yonder." The fact that the body is now in the ground and the soul of the deceased has departed is more than we like to admit.

In asking if one's father is still living, the Chinese say, "Is your father still located?" The reply would be, "He's located," or "He's not located," whichever is the case. The word "death" is rarely used, even in the world's most ancient culture.

Today we are confronted with so many voices telling us how to live. We are told how to look young, stay trim, keep healthy, have a good image, think positively, make more money, have more friends. All these are reasonable ambitions, but they indicate that we are trying desperately to cling to this present world. The truth is, life is transitory. "What is your life? You are a mist that appears for a little while and then vanishes" (James 4:14b). The psalmist said, "Each man's life is but a breath"

(Psalm 39:5). If we want to make the most of life, we need to face the fact that it is going to end.

My father-in-law, Dr. L. Nelson Bell, wrote many years ago, "Only those who are prepared to die are really prepared to live." The uncertainty is not the dying, it's the preparation.

Facing Reality

If we are in a battle with this enemy called Death, I believe we should learn about it, in order to know how to confront the dying experience. We need to know how to face that enemy on our own behalf, and how to deal with the inevitable deaths of loved ones and friends.

Can you imagine any military strategist saying, "Well, if there really is an enemy out there, perhaps I should find out something about him . . . later"? It reminds me of the situation at the beginning of World War II. As long as history is recorded, the attack on Pearl Harbor on December 7, 1941, will be remembered. The Japanese High Command code-named the attack "Operation Z," and its planning took place more than a year before the launch of warplanes that would destroy the battleships and aircraft carriers at Pearl Harbor, the heart of the U.S. Pacific Fleet.

In the summer of 1941 I went to Washington, D.C., with my wife Ruth's family. Dr. Bell was intent on meeting with officials at the State Department to alert them to an imminent Japanese attack. He was politely ignored. Other warnings had been heard, but also went unheeded; America was unprepared for what happened at Pearl Harbor, blindly refusing to face the encroaching danger.

Can we afford to ignore the warnings of our ultimate enemy? We need to break the conspiracy of silence
about the subject with a biblically sound, realistic approach. Years ago there was a popular play called "Death
Takes a Holiday." The idea was provocative and made
good drama with its impossible theme; however, while
death was not a part of God's original plan, we cannot
escape it. Death *never* takes a holiday (with one possible
exception which we will consider later).

Adolescents are notorious for denying the reality of
death; it is the farthest thing from their minds. In the
vigor of youth, they take life for granted, and perhaps
they should at that age; but all of us tend to take life for
granted when times are good, when there is plenty, when
the economy is strong, when things are getting better.
Death is the last thing on our minds when we have full
stomachs. But let a person who is reasonably intelligent
ponder slightly the reality of death and that person is on
his or her way to an existential crisis. That person starts
asking questions like, "Who am I?" "Why am I here?"
"Where am I going from here?" Sometimes the questions
come on the heels of a serious setback or sudden loss,
when the good times disappear, when the party's over,
and he or she has to face the morning after. If the individual has a mind and feelings, there is no way to deny
the reality.

There are signs that some people are trying to develop a more informed approach to the subject. In fact,
some educators are saying death has come out of the
closet and into the classroom. I have been told that sex is
the only subject which is more popular on the campus
these days. Students are visiting morgues, even making
their own funeral arrangements. For whatever reasons,

death as a topic is in vogue, but the mature Christian perspective is still something less than hot news.

I suspect that modern society, with the potential for nuclear incineration, military holocaust, and natural disaster puts the spotlight on the subject for these young people. But I also suspect that the constant bombardment of TV violence is a factor.

Discussing death scientifically may help us become more capable of discussing the personal aspects of dying; and facing the fact of our own death can help us cope with our neurotic fears of dying. But most important, we can come to grips with the need to get our life's priorities in order. However, we cannot begin to understand the riddle of death without the guiding knowledge of the Word of God. Outside of the Bible, death will forever remain an unknown phantom, stalking helpless human victims.

Throughout this book it is my desire to approach the fact of death objectively and compassionately as God has revealed it to us through the Scriptures.

Although death is, as the apostle Paul claimed, the last enemy, one of the main purposes of this book is to show that it need not be feared.

Death: Our Mortal Enemy

The Bible stresses that death is an enemy, not a friend—both of God and of us.

Why is death our enemy? I'm not thinking of the death which is a release from pain, debilitating disease, or advanced age, but death the enemy who snatches a child before he learns to play in the sunshine. It is the enemy who takes the young couple before they can be married, stops the youth who wants to be a pilot, or kills the young father and leaves orphaned children and a destitute wife. As you read this sentence, one person will die. Death, like an unfinished symphony, leaves fragments of many promising careers and lives.

One woman wrote me about the death of her husband. She called it an "untimely death."

"He had called me twice that morning," she said, "after supposedly recovering after a week's stay for heart treatment in the hospital. He told me he was 'coming home.' The doctor scheduled him for a 'mild' treadmill test, and thirty minutes later the hospital called to say he died on the treadmill. The shock has been almost unbearable. Please pray that I will be able to accept this part of the Lord's plan."

Although we think of the death of a young person, or one in the prime of life, as being the most difficult for loved ones, that is not always true. I heard from one woman who said, "Please pray for me, I feel so lost without my husband. He was my life. We were married for sixty years."

Frank Coy was in Cleveland talking to his wife by long distance telephone to their home near Phoenix, Arizona. She had not been feeling very well. Frank and Virginia were extremely close and had been married for many years. They had looked forward to his retirement as president of the May Company in Cleveland, and were traveling about the country, though he still served on many boards including ours. During the conversation she said she had a pain. He said, "Well, honey, I think you ought to go to the hospital." All of a sudden he heard the phone drop. He immediately called a hospital in Phoenix and within four minutes the paramedics were there, but it was too late. She had died while talking to her husband on the phone. It absolutely crushed Frank. Except for the companionship of the Lord, he seems to be totally lost without Virginia. Heaven is much closer to him now.

Death: Enemy of God's Plan

"But, Lord. I don't want to die." And the Lord, as it were, answers: I didn't plan the world that way, but someday, even this enemy will be destroyed. God reminds us of that through the apostle Paul. "For he must reign until he has put all his enemies under his feet. The last enemy to be destroyed is death" (1 Corinthians 15:25, 26).

Why is death an enemy of God? Because it destroys life, in contrast to God, the creator and author of life. In fact, the Bible tells us that neither sin nor pain, disease nor death were part of God's original plan for man. Death was the penalty for sin, and Adam and Eve made the choice of their own free wills. When they did not obey God, He told the first man and woman if they ate from the fruit of the tree of the knowledge of good and evil, they would die. But Satan scoffed at God's warning and told them they surely would not die. Adam and Eve chose to ignore God's warning and to believe Satan's lie. "For the wages of sin is death, but the gift of God is eternal life in Christ Jesus our Lord" (Romans 6:23).

Death is the common lot of every human being and of every other living thing—both plants and animals. Sin and death, the Bible tells us, have afflicted the whole of God's creation, including the natural world, and only when Christ comes in His glory at the end of the present era will sin be eradicated and creation be restored to God's original plan. "The creation waits in eager expectation for the sons of God to be revealed. For the creation was subjected to frustration, not by its own choice, but by the will of the one who subjected it, in hope that the creation itself will be liberated from its bondage to decay and brought into the glorious freedom of the children of God" (Romans 8:19–21).

Did you ever wonder what would have happened to man if he hadn't sinned? We certainly don't know, because the Scriptures don't tell us. But perhaps man would have been translated to heaven without passing through death, just as Enoch and Elijah were. There *will* be a generation of believers who will not know physical death. Those who are still alive when Jesus Christ returns in glory for His own will not die but will be changed "in a flash, in the twinkling of an eye" (1 Corinthians 15:52).

A child asked his mother, "Where would I be if I hadn't been born?" How can we answer that? It's like asking what would have happened if Eve hadn't taken a bite of the forbidden fruit and Adam hadn't succumbed to her invitation. We just don't know.

Some Reactions to Death

People encounter death from different perspectives. Some defy death, as did my friend Steve McQueen, until it consumed him with cancer. They laugh at death, as did Will Rogers, until the day his plane crashed. George Burns says, "I don't believe in death." But they invite death when life becomes unbearable, as did Marilyn Monroe. Sometimes they are resigned to death, as was the hapless Anne Boleyn, second queen consort of Henry VIII. She wrote these poignant final words:

Oh, death, rock me asleep! Bring me to quiet and rest
Let me pass my weary, guiltless life
   out of my careful breast.
Toll on the passing bell, ring out my doleful knell;
Let thy sound my death tell; Death doth draw me,
Death doth draw me; There is no remedy.[2]

Still others have a fatalistic attitude toward death or reject it, claiming we should not worry about it because there is no life after death and there is nothing we can do about death anyway.

The Greek philosopher, Epicurus, lived three centuries before Christ and wrote in a seriocomic tone about death, as we have a tendency to do when we are nervous about a subject. He said, "Death, feared as the most awful of evils, is really nothing. For so long as we are, death has not come, and when it has come we are not."

Others go to the opposite extreme and live in constant, paralyzing fear of death. Because they have no security and assurance of God's love and protection in the midst of death, their lives are preoccupied with fear and often filled with attempts to win God's favor and avoid His anger.

Christians are not immune to the fear of death. Death is not always a "beautiful release," but an enemy which separates. There is a certain mystery to it. It does not respect the young or the old, the good or the evil, the Christian or the heathen.

Our individual responses to death cannot be placed in neat categories and given labels. However, our experiences with life and death are generally similar to those of others around us. The Bible says, "No temptation has seized you except what is common to man" (1 Corinthians 10:13).

But we need not give way to defiance, or rejection, or fear, or any of the other attitudes people adopt in the face of the reality of death. There is another way—the way of Christ—by which we know that while the experience of death is certain, so also is the fact of heaven. For the Christian, death can be faced realistically and with victory, because he knows that "neither death nor life, neither angels nor demons, neither the present nor the future, nor any powers, neither height nor depth, nor anything else in all creation, will be able to separate us from the love of God that is in Christ Jesus our Lord" (Romans 8:38–39).

Now, I am not anxious to die, nor am I writing this book with any knowledge of my imminent departure. And just because the Bible tells us that believers have a blessed hope of conquering death, we don't run to the door and say to the enemy, "Come on in, I've been waiting anxiously for you." It is not a sign of weak faith for the Christian to face death with reluctance. The apostle Paul confessed that he was torn between the desire to die and be with Christ and the need to continue his work in the churches. He wrote to the believers in Philippi, "I am torn between the two: I desire to depart and be with Christ, which is better by far; but it is more necessary for you that I remain in the body" (Philippians 1:23, 24).

Can we be realistic, without being morbid? Can we find peace, assurance, triumph, and even humor, in a subject which is avoided by many but vitally important and inevitable to everyone? I am convinced we can.

2

DEATH: NO

MORE TABOOS

"Now that the taboo has been lifted, it is more important than ever for Christians to get involved in some of the great questions about the process of dying. The Bible has the answers to the fear of death, but we need the principles in God's Word about the dying experience."

There is a time for everything, and a season for every activity under heaven: a time to be born and a time to die. . . .

Ecclesiastes 3:1, 2

I majored in anthropology in college. That may not seem to be a good educational foundation for a clergyman. At the time, however, I thought it would give me a greater understanding of other cultures and peoples, never dreaming how useful it would become when my future ministry would be worldwide.

It is fascinating to me how customs and traditions reflect the way people really think. Hold a mirror to history and we see the art, music, literature, and manners of each era. Sometimes those of us who have lived five or more decades reach the stage where we shake our heads and say, "In my day it was different." Of course it was. And someday our children may mimic us when they tell our grandchildren, "When I was your age . . . ."

29

Attitudes toward death have changed more than styles in clothing. We have passed from the ceremonial to the unmentionable and have reached the present "gloom boom." More books have been written about death in the last ten years than in the previous century.

A few hundred years ago, death was a ritual. Knowing that his end was near, the dying person prepared for death, as Sir Lancelot did in the Knights of the Round Table. After he was wounded in battle he believed he was about to die. He spread out his arms, his body forming a cross. He turned his head so that he faced east, toward Jerusalem. He was ready for death.

Death had its own protocol. If the dying person was unable to remember what it was, those present would remind him what the proper custom was. One historian who carefully studied the attitudes toward death in the Middle Ages, wrote, "The dying man, according to Guillaume Durand, bishop of Mende, must lie on his back so that his face is always turned toward heaven."[1]

Today on television our dying heroes fall over with a few "ughs!" if allowed that much. They jerk, explode, or topple over with no chance to leave another generation quotable words. "His last words were . . ." has been replaced by the gut reaction.

In the more romantic tradition of the past, phrases such as Hamlet's words, "To be or not to be, that is the question," masked the ugliness of death in lyrical language.

Deathbed scenes in past centuries were a public ceremony, many times including friends, relatives, and children. Illustrations in old books frequently pictured a high canopied bed on which rested the wasted form of its occupant surrounded by people in various stages of grief, concern, or even indifference. A dying man's bedroom was like Grand Central Station. However, toward the end of the eighteenth century, physicians were increasingly concerned with basic principles of hygiene and were unhappy about overcrowded conditions in the bedrooms of the dying.

Those final days when a person needed to commune with God or with loved ones were regarded as a right for the dying. People prepared to die. The language of wills documented a person's careful last plan, including his statement of faith. For instance, here is what Patrick Henry wrote in his will:

I have now disposed of all my property to my family. There is one thing more I wish I could give them, and that is faith in Jesus Christ. If they had that and I had not given them one shilling, they would be rich; and if I had not given them that, and had given them all the world, they would be poor indeed.

However, the second half of the eighteenth century saw a considerable change in wills. "The pious clauses, the choice of a tomb, the funding of religious services, and the giving of alms all disappeared; the will was reduced to the document we find today, a legal act distributing the estate, small or large. Thus the will was completely secularized . . . ."[2]

The historian commented, "It has been thought that this secularization was one of the signs of the de-Christianization of society."

What interests me is that the return to the concept of Christian wills is being seen in our day.

In the nineteenth century came a new preoccupation

with the decor of death. There were funeral proces-
sions, mourning clothes, the spread of cemeteries, regu-
lar visits, and pilgrimages to tombs. There was a pomp
connected with the departure from life which was elaborate and prolonged.

But customs changed. As the twentieth century,
with its rapid changes in technology, communication, and
lifestyles, began its breathless race into the future, death
became an unmentionable topic (perhaps due in part to
increasing secularism). Over a period of time, people
began to exclude children from deathbed scenes, or even
viewing the dead. Death became a private affair; eventually even the family was excluded as the hospitalization of
the terminally ill became widespread.

With this came the rejection of mourning during
much of this century. The community felt less and less
involved in the death of its members. Geoffrey Gorer, an
Englishman, began a study of this change in attitudes
toward death and mourning as a result of a series of
personal experiences. He lost his father on the *Lusitania*
in 1915, so was never able to see his body. It was 1931
before he first viewed a dead body and could experience
and observe the conventions of mourning. However, in
the late 1940s he experienced the deaths of two close
friends, and was struck by the rejection of traditional
ways of mourning. In 1955 he published an article called
"The Pornography of Death." In it, he showed how death
had become as shameful in the modern age as sex was
to the Victorians. One taboo had been substituted for
another.

Children were excluded from funeral services,
sometimes even those of their own parents. Gorer, reflecting on his own life, told about the death of his

brother in 1961. In speaking of his nephews he said, "Their father's death was quite unmarked for them by ritual of any kind, and was even nearly treated as a secret, for it was many months before Elizabeth (his wife) could bear to mention him or have him mentioned in her presence."[3]

In a questionnaire published by *Psychology Today* in 1971, a woman of twenty-five wrote, "When I was twelve, my mother died of leukemia. She was there when I went to bed and when I woke up the next morning, my parents were gone. My father came home, took my brother and me on his knee, and burst into screeching sobs and said, 'Jesus took your mother.' Then we never talked about it again. It was too painful for all of us."[4]

How unfortunate it is when Jesus is depicted to children as the person who "took" mommy or daddy, without the child having a previous understanding of the hope of heaven and eternal life. It is no wonder that the young woman just mentioned had to undergo counseling therapy in later years.

In contrast, my wife Ruth tells about the death of her former Wheaton College roommate, Ann King Blocher, who died surrounded by her husband and all five of her children. Another friend, Helen Morken, was dying of cancer when she said to Ruth in a telephone conversation that "The prayers of God's people are the extension of His loving arms." Ruth sent her a cassette of hymns and sacred music she had put together for her own mother and later produced for distribution, called "Looking Homeward." Helen played it by the hour. As she died, her entire family stood around her bed and literally sang her into the glory of heaven.

Whatever Happened to Hell?

As attitudes toward death and dying changed, another significant shift began to take place within the human family. The reality of Satan was ignored increasingly or discarded as a myth. Even many who believed in a personal devil were not allowed to acknowledge his power in this world, nor did they believe in hell.

Hell, in the eyes of unbelievers and even some believers, was abandoned. Or it was relegated to some vague concept of "evil in the world." Even some theologians chose to reject the Bible's clear teaching on hell.

Certainly war, hunger, terrorism, greed, and hatred are hell on earth, but, except for the Bible believer, a future hell became part of the ash heap of ancient history. As hell was becoming for many no more than a swear word, sin was also an accepted way of life. People began to look to science, education, and social and moral programs as possible solutions to the growing chaos of an insane world. If people can ignore what the Bible calls sin, then they can quite logically discount what it says about the reality of hell.

Whoever chooses to deny that there is a hell must then face certain questions. "Where do I go when I die?" "Who goes to heaven, and who doesn't?" And, "If I don't go to heaven, what is the alternative?"

In contemporary society hell is not a popular subject. George Gallup made a survey on hell and there were some interesting results. In his national poll 53 percent of the general population of the United States said they believe in hell. The percentage goes down dramatically among people with a college education and those with high incomes. Simply stated, the Gallup poll showed that the more education and money people had, the less likely they were to believe in hell.

What about heaven? In the Gallup survey, 66 percent of the general population said they believe in "a heaven where people who have led good lives are eternally rewarded." More people are confident that there is a heaven than are concerned about hell. I was especially interested that those who believed in heaven were asked a further question, "How would you describe your own chances of going to heaven—excellent, good, fair, or poor?"

Among the Protestant denominations, only 26 percent of the Baptists, 20 percent of the Lutherans, and 16 percent of the Methodists thought their chances of attaining heaven were excellent. The survey further revealed that while only 24 percent of the Protestants said they were sure of a place in heaven, 41 percent of the Catholics had this assurance.[5]

Why did members of organized churches, or those professing to be either Protestant or Catholic, have such a low assurance of heaven? Could it be that in our descriptions of heaven we have failed to mention the horrors of its alternative? Have we overreacted to the old "hell-fire and brimstone" preaching by discarding or at least watering down the clear teaching of the Bible? Jesus spoke of hell as "darkness, where there will be weeping and gnashing of teeth" (Matthew 8:12). Or have we even neglected the whole question of life after death by emphasizing only this life?

Jesus used the strongest words possible to describe the horrors of hell.

Having traveled widely and spoken with multitudes

of people in many countries where the Christian faith is no longer as strong as it once was, I was not surprised to learn from the Gallup poll that more Americans believe in hell than do those in any of the other countries where Christianity is the major organized religion. In Sweden, for instance, only 17 percent believe in hell; France, 22 percent; Great Britain, 23 percent; West Germany, 25 percent; Switzerland, 25 percent; the Netherlands, 28 percent. Other countries in Europe were equally low.

Gallup surmises, and I tend to agree, that some of the reasons why more people believe in heaven than in hell is that "Hell is like death—people try not to think about it."[6] Jackie Gleason appearing on "60 Minutes" with Morley Safer indicated that he believed there was eternal life ahead either in heaven or hell. I remember talking to Jackie on several occasions in years past on this very theme.

Just because people do not believe in hell doesn't mean it doesn't exist! Jesus warned, "Be afraid of the one who can destroy both soul and body in hell" (Matthew 10:28). If there is no hell, then Jesus lied.

Some people who believe in the passages in the Bible about heaven, utterly reject the references to hell. Robert Ingersoll, a famous lawyer and atheist in the latter part of the nineteenth century, once delivered a blistering lecture on hell. He called hell the "scarecrow of religion" and told his audience how unscientific it was, and how all intelligent people had decided there was no such place. A drunk in the audience came up to him afterward and said, "Bob, I liked your lecture; I liked what you said about hell. But, Bob, I want you to be sure about it, because I'm depending on you."[7]

In World War I, British soldiers had a popular song that went like this:

> Oh Death, where is thy sting-a-ling-a-ling,
> Oh Grave, thy victoree?
> The bells of Hell go ting-a-ling-a-ling
> For you but not for me.[8]

A lot of people talk about hell, use it to tell others where to go, but do not want to be confronted with the thought that it might be their destination. Hell, for them, is only where the Hitlers and Stalins should end up, along with murderers, rapists, or child pornographers. But most think that "Good People" who mind their own business, pay their taxes, and put a few dollars in the collection plate will have some "eternal rewards."

However, if the Bible is true, we know there is abundant life after death for the followers of Christ. Those who have accepted His grace and been saved will be with Him in heaven. And what about the others? "Surely a loving God would not punish good people!" says the humanitarian or the religious person who wants to ignore the uncomfortable and unpopular descriptions of hell in the Bible. Yes, they are right in some ways, for a loving God does not want anyone to perish. The Lord is not slow in keeping His promise, as some understand slowness. "He is patient with you, not wanting anyone to perish, but everyone to come to repentance" (2 Peter 3:9).

However, the Scriptures are very clear. Jesus told His disciples not to fear the killers of men, because they only cause physical death. He did not mean, of course, that we are not to be concerned about murderers, but His point was a warning of something more serious than the death of our bodies. Jesus said, "But I will show you whom you should fear: Fear him who, after the killing of the body, has power to throw you into hell" (Luke 12:5).

Let's clarify a few things about that verse in Luke. First of all, it refers to God, not to Satan; for Satan cannot determine the destiny of a human soul.

Also, I know many people stumble over the idea of "fearing God." Fear does not imply a crippling dread, but a healthy, reverent respect. All through the Bible we read about fearing the Lord. If we substitute "have deep reverence for," we may be closer to understanding the meaning of the word.

The problem is not that hell exists, because it must if God is holy and we distinguish between the biblical meaning of good and evil. The problem is that men don't understand how evil sin is in the eyes of a supremely holy God. Sin is not rated on a sliding scale, like a report card. Sin is eternal separation from God and can only be pardoned by a truly supreme sacrifice: the death of the Son of God, on the cross.

In Our Time

Today the dying experience is more openly discussed; however, many of the accounts I've heard or read of those last moments tend to confuse the biblical doctrines and raise more questions than they answer. A good example is the popularity of accounts of "near-death" experiences, in which a person claims to have approached death (or even died) and then come back to life.

It is not my purpose to doubt the sincerity of those people who have recounted their "out-of-body" experiences.

Many describe near-death encounters after a cardiac arrest or other medical crisis and tell how they seemed to rise and watch as the medical team tried to revive them. Nor do I question those who tell about seeing spirits of relatives and friends who have already died, or others who have encountered a "being of light" which brings them through a tunnel into an overwhelming, ecstatic experience of such intensity that they find it difficult to describe. I have heard many such stories offered in vivid detail, and, without exception, these life-after-death experiences seem to reduce the fear of dying.

Most of the supernatural experiences we hear or read about have classic similarities. The person who is "dead" (and we'll discuss the meaning of that word shortly) rises out of his or her body, hears strange sounds, seems to be going down a long, dark tunnel and recognizes himself hovering somewhere between life and death, and then encounters someone or something in white, or a diffusion of light. Those who return from this journey are changed persons.

These kinds of stories are not an American phenomenon. They are described by people of other cultures and nations. In addition, psychic literature and cultic practices are full of such occurrences.

U.S. News and World Report, July 11, 1983, said, "While critics have labeled these experiences mere dreams, fabrications or hallucinations brought on by pain-killing drugs or release of chemicals in the brain, at least a half-dozen books have been written attempting to give scientific evidence of the phenomenon. The International Association for Near Death Studies also has been set up at the University of Connecticut to foster research in this area. Whatever the explanation, we know from extensive studies that something extraordinarily interesting happens to many people at the moment of death, says Connecticut Psychologist Kenneth Ring, who stresses that near-death experiences do not prove the existence of an afterlife but merely show that the act of dying may not be the agonizing event many people fear."

But these experiences are not the bases for eternal truths nor are they a solid foundation for our confidence in life after death. They may be dangerously deceptive. They must be examined in the context of God's Word.

The Bible does prove there is life after death and the biblical explanation of death is very clear. Each man dies once, and there are two possible results and destinations. "Just as man is destined to die once, and after that to face judgment" (Hebrews 9:27). What bothers me about the life-after-death stories is that regardless of whether the person is a believer or not, seldom in these experiences does death appear to have any negative consequences—which is a direct contradiction of the Bible's teaching. If all death experiences are the same, there is no judgment or hell, and the Word of God is a lie. We do not presently know for certain what the source is for these "out of body" experiences. Some have even suggested they are sometimes satanic in origin, since they can deceive people about the true nature of death and salvation, and (in this view) are a satanic counterfeit of the Christian's assurance of heavenly rest.

The desire to gain a better understanding of death has been called the "new obsession." I certainly don't want to be unbalanced in thinking about the subject, but I am convinced that when we know where death leads, we will know the "hope of glory" spoken of by Paul in Colossians 1:27.

What Is Death, Anyway?

"Can doctors agree with God on the time to die?" This difficult question was asked by an assistant professor in the Department of Medicine, Medical College of Wisconsin. Many of us will be confronted with that question and we need to face it with an understanding of its complexity.

The Bible tells us precisely what death is. Physical death is separation of the spirit and soul from the body: ". . . the body without the spirit is dead" (James 2:26). But there is a far worse death, and that is spiritual death. Spiritual death is separation from God.

To the materialistic thinker, death means complete annihilation. For the Hindu and the Buddhist, death means reincarnation. To the terrorist, death provides a way to be rewarded for his cause. Many Shiite Moslems believe that for every infidel they kill (especially Christians and Jews), they will have incomparable sexual pleasures in paradise.

Today, the whole question of "when is a person dead" is being discussed more ardently than at any other time in recent history. A relatively new discipline called thanatology (from the Greek *thanatos,* or death) has entered our language and classrooms. Thanatology is the study, or science, of death.

Making his investigation of death and dying in America today, David Dempsey wrote that "Our society has secularized life. In so doing it has removed death from its traditional religious context, the belief that it is part of the natural order of things. When death was viewed more theologically, when suffering itself was thought of as spiritually purifying, when men believed

41

in some kind of afterlife that justified suffering, death was more acceptable."[9]

What is death? One man who has stood beside hundreds of dying persons is Chaplain Phil Manly, a compassionate man who has served at the University of Southern California Medical Center in Los Angeles for many years. With his beeper always on his belt, he is on call for any doctor whose patient is terminally ill. He has held the hands of men, women, and children at the moment of their deaths, and consoled loved ones in the midst of their grief. On the wall of his cramped office, which is in one of the largest medical facilities in the world (a center which employs some eight thousand people), Chaplain Manly keeps a chart of the number of deaths each day. He describes the medical definitions which most experts would use to pronounce a person dead.

Clinical death is when the heart stops beating, blood pressure is unreadable, and the body temperature drops. It is generally agreed that a patient is dead when the vital functions utterly fail.

Sure death is the total absence of brainwave activity. A committee of physicians, lawyers, theologians, and scientists at Harvard determined what was to be considered "brain death." Four criteria were listed:

1. Unreceptivity and unresponsivity
2. No movements or breathing
3. No reflexes
4. Flat electroencephalogram[10]

The most complete definition of death seems to be "an irreversible loss of the vital functions." Death, then, is defined as the state in which physical resuscitation is impossible.

Not all physicians, lawyers, and laymen agree, however, on the definitions for the precise moment or process of death.

To complicate matters, some people have been resuscitated who were considered "clinically dead." A friend of mine was in a hospital in Tucson with pulmonary fibrosis and Russian flu. Three times during his stay in the intensive care unit he stopped breathing and had all of the signs of being "clinically dead." Three times he was revived by a mechanical respirator. When he was released from the hospital, the headline in the *Arizona Daily Star* said, "Nearly dead, now he's home, and nurses believe in miracles."

We know that doctors can often postpone death. The American Medical Association says, "The social commitment of the physician is to sustain life and relieve suffering" (*AMA Judicial Counsel*, March 1986). Today, even doctors struggle with decisions about when to sustain life.

Those who have been brought back to life after being considered dead include more than just the current examples of medical wizardry. For instance, Elijah revived a child whose "sickness was so severe, that there was no breath left in him" (1 Kings 17:17 NASB). In fact, faithful Elijah could have used what we call artificial respiration on the boy, because it says that he "stretched himself upon the child three times, and called to the Lord, and said, Oh Lord my God, I pray Thee, let this child's life return to him" (1 Kings 17:21 NASB).

Elisha was another biblical character who never had a Red Cross CPR course. Yet he went into the home of the lad who was laid out on his bed and proclaimed dead, prayed, and then "went up and lay on the child, and put his mouth on his mouth and his eyes on his eyes and his hands on his hands, and he stretched himself on him; and the flesh of the child became warm" (2 Kings 4:34 NASB).

I have the greatest respect for the medical profession, having been in the competent care of fine doctors, especially at the Mayo Clinic where I get my annual physical. However, I also realize that sometimes they are in the unenviable position of not being able to determine a true definition of death. While the physicians cannot have the final power over death, they can achieve temporary power over it. This is the doctor's dilemma—and the patient's, too.

Sometimes the issues of death become so complicated that we are again reminded of Job's question in the midst of all his extreme suffering. He asked, "But where can wisdom be found? Where does understanding dwell? Man does not comprehend its worth; it cannot be found in the land of the living" (Job 28:12, 13).

Here is a sample of the many instances where man's wisdom is severely taxed:

In 1968, a sixty-two-year-old man named John Stuckwish received a transplanted heart from Dr. Denton Cooley and his team at St. Luke's Hospital in Houston. The donor was a thirty-six-year-old man named Clarence Nicks. Nicks' brain had been damaged beyond any possibility of returning to its normal functions by a beating he had received at the hands of a group of attackers. There were no signs of electrical activity in the brain and there was no spontaneous respiration. It is critical, however, that his heart continued to beat for some time. Dr. Cooley and his team took the heart from Nicks' body and placed it in that of Mr.

Stuckwish. The ethical questions arise when one begins to reflect on the relationship of the surgeon, the donor, and the donor's attackers. The people who beat up this donor have now been arrested. They pleaded in their defense that Nicks was not dead at the time the heart was given; his heart was still beating. The attackers even went beyond that to accuse the physician who removed the heart of murdering Nicks. To complicate matters, one physician had pronounced Nicks dead at the time his brain stopped and his respiratory functions stopped, while another physician specifically disagreed.[11]

Surely, the definition of physical death is a complicated, delicate decision—and I would not pretend to give a final scientific answer to that question. We know God may occasionally add time to a person's life, even when others determine he has gone. What some may think is the conclusion of a life may only be the closing of a chapter, not the end of the book. For instance, in the Old Testament, King Hezekiah was mortally ill, but the Lord said He would heal him and add fifteen years to his life. Jesus brought the daughter of Jairus back to life, and Lazarus was raised from the dead after being in his tomb for four days.

I believe God allows physicians to use their modern technology to extend physical life today in a way that is unprecedented in human history. I am constantly in awe of the tenacious qualities in the human spirit, and also of the ability of skilled physicians to treat crisis after crisis and somehow manage to pull the patient through. At the same time death is a reality, and is still the ultimate event we must all face.

Is it any wonder that people study, discuss, and evaluate death today? A young minister told about a series of seminars that were held in a Los Angeles church. Out of the five different subject areas offered, the one with the largest attendance dealt with "Death and Dying." At the University of Southern California, a very popular course is "Religious and Ethical Issues in Death and Dying." *U.S. News and World Report* did a special report on "A New Understanding about Death" (July 11, 1983).

Now that the taboo has been lifted, it is more important than ever for Christians to get involved in some of the great questions about the process of dying. The Bible has the answer to the fear of death, but we also need to understand and apply the principles in God's Word about the dying experience.

The time to understand is now, while we are healthy and alert. Those in the mental health field, the philosophers, psychologists, sociologists, and even physicians, do not have the answers. The Bible says, "so that your faith might not rest on men's wisdom, but on God's power" (1 Corinthians 2:5).

John Trapp, a great theologian from England, lived over three hundred years ago. He said, "There is a perfect time for a man to die, which, if he knew all there was to know about life he would choose that time and no other."

Thank God that we can have an open, realistic discussion of death. We need the wisdom of God to live our complicated lives, and even more so for the inevitable conclusion.

3

KING OF

TERRORS

"The truth is that all of us have our time to die, and the conspiracy of silence that so often surrounds death today cannot change that fact . . . within most of us is a strong desire to hold on to physical life as long as possible."

He is torn from the security of his tent and marched off to the king of terrors.

Job 18:14

———————————

The conversation at the party became hushed as someone reported that a friend had just been told he had incurable cancer. A psychiatrist—a strong, handsome man who was a prominent member of the social and professional community—said, "I'm scared to death of dying." He smiled sheepishly at his feeble pun, but he had honestly expressed what so many people feel.

In spite of rapid and ever-increasing advances in medical technology and pain relief, no one has found a way to lessen people's fear of dying. This is not some new psychosis but a condition as old as man. David, the bold youth who defied the giant Goliath, the king who pursued his enemies and destroyed them, is the same man who cried out, "My heart is in anguish within me; the terrors of death assail me. Fear and trembling have beset me; horror has overwhelmed me" (Psalm 55:4, 5).

Age and circumstances often dictate the degree of fear a person may feel when facing death. David did not say those words when he was a teenager facing Goliath, but when he was older and had experienced sickness and betrayal by friends. Sometimes the fear of death grows significantly with age.

Jesus' disciples were rugged men, physically toughened by living outdoors and traveling long distances on foot. And yet when they were caught in a sudden storm so common in the area of Galilee, they shouted in desperate fear, "Lord, save us! We are going to drown!" (Matthew 8:25). They were terrified that they were going to die.

My friend, Jack Black, has defined fear as "an emotion that speaks of dread, fright, alarm, panic, trepidation, and consternation." All human beings capable of thinking manifest these emotions. Thus, fear is universal in all times and places. It is a normal, human response to the unknown. And death, the experience of death, is an unknown.

Is there more fear of death today than there was before technology enabled us to prolong life? Many people think so—although we try (as we have seen) to hide it or suppress it. Some psychiatrists say that fear of death fosters a variety of psychoses. Others believe that fear is intensified by the medical emergencies which cause them to be treated more like a thing than a human.

Another indication that the fear of death has become more prevalent comes from the fact that 80 percent of the people in the United States die in hospitals or convalescent centers instead of at home. Dying can be a lonely business. David Dempsey says, "Most hospitals in this country share at least two characteristics: they do their best to conceal from the patient the fact that he might be dying, and when the fateful time draws near they isolate him from family and friends."[1]

Conspiracy of Silence

Some believe that telling the truth to a person who may be dying is destructive to his morale. The patient's resigned comment, "I think I'm going to die," may likely be met by the reassuring deception, "Now don't talk like that. You'll probably outlive us all." This kind of deception is practiced by medical personnel as well as by family, thinking they are being kind and acting in the patient's best interest. The "conspiracy of silence" is based upon the assumption that people don't want to think about death, especially their own. However, studies indicate that most people *are* willing to think and talk about dying, even though they may be frightened by the idea. Certainly I wouldn't want anyone to give me forced cheerfulness when what I need is honesty and love.

My wife Ruth told me about a pastor's wife who was dying of cancer. She knew it, and so did her family. But they kept telling her she was going to recover. One day a friend called on her, and the sick woman said, "I know I'm dying, but nobody will talk to me about it. Please tell me about heaven." For more than an hour they had a marvelous time, laughing and talking about her heavenly home.

Another woman told me about a visit with her brother who was in an isolation ward in intensive care.

She was gowned and masked to help shield him from possible infection, so he could not see her smile or feel the touch of her hand. Nor could he move from one position because of the tubes attached to his body. She thought she should keep a positive attitude, so she said to him, "You're going to walk out of here someday, Bert." Tears flooded his eyes as he shook his head feebly and pointed one finger up. He was trying to tell her that he was on his way to heaven.

The man died two days later and his sister said she regretted she hadn't given him reassuring words about his eternal home, rather than offering him false expectations. There is a fine line between hope and compassionate honesty. Only the wisdom of God can guide us in moments like these.

The truth is that all of us have our time to die. The conspiracy of silence which so often surrounds death today cannot change that fact. Of course, within most of us is a strong desire to hold on to physical life as long as possible. I could relate many of the stories I've heard about how the timing of death is often determined by a person's desire to live for a certain goal. One of my friends told me that when he and his wife, Joannie, were on an extended trip in Europe, his wife's father in Illinois was given only a few days to live. He rallied long enough to say, "I want to see Joannie again." He asked that his daughter and son-in-law not be told how serious his condition was, because he didn't want to spoil their trip. They returned home as scheduled, and ten days later her father died peacefully in his daughter's loving arms.

A sociologist, David Phillips of the State University of New York at Stony Brook, reported that terminally ill people tend to hang onto life until they reach some date that is important to them—a wedding anniversary, a birthday, a religious holiday. "This appears to be particularly true for the famous because of the attention they receive on such occasions. Phillips found that these notables were less likely to die in the months preceding their birthdays, and more likely to die in the three months following them. It is interesting, for instance, that both Thomas Jefferson and John Adams died on July 4, fifty years to the day after they had signed the Declaration of Independence."[2]

I remember when I heard of the death of Corrie ten Boom, the remarkable Dutch woman who hid Jews from the Gestapo during World War II and later was sent to the infamous Ravensbruck concentration camp. Her sister died in camp, but Corrie was released, and for more than thirty years she traveled the world, telling her experiences and writing books. Corrie's story received national attention in the movie, *The Hiding Place*, and in the many books she wrote. For the last few years of her life her friends and co-workers made quite an occasion of her birthdays. She was bedridden and unable to speak for the last five years of her life, but she truly loved parties. Corrie died on her ninety-first birthday, April 15, 1983. As one friend said, "What a birthday party she must have had!"

Corrie died in God's good time, at the end of a long life lived for the glory of God.

On the other hand, there are many who die prematurely, having reached a point in their lives when they feel they have no more goals left. Idle retired people reportedly have a shorter life span than those who continue with purposeful activity. We have all heard stories of a bereaved husband or wife surviving less than a year after the death of a spouse. When love is gone, life is gone. And unless we can feel needed by someone, life seems meaningless.

David Dempsey's study relates that "one survey of 260 persons sixty and over found that only 10 percent answered the question, 'Are you afraid to die?' in the affirmative. The authors believe that the high percentage of those who said they were not afraid can be accounted for by an almost as high (77 percent) number of persons who professed a belief in some kind of after-life."[3]

That is an interesting statistic. It shows the peace of mind we gain through faith, even when the vigor of life is somewhat diminished. The challenge we have as believers is to do our best to ensure that the "afterlife" in which so many put their trust is the genuine article and not a false front, like a house on a movie set.

The fear of death is not universal. Many factors such as age, physical health, family, social, and religious backgrounds make a difference. There are times when you hear people say, "Oh, I wish I could die." And yet, after a bout in the hospital or a near brush with death, the same person might say, "It's great to be alive!"

More than likely it is the process of dying that frightens people—not death itself. Chaplain Phil Manly said that as a hospital chaplain he has seen many people die very peacefully. Physicians have told me that while the body is fighting for survival, there may be severe suffering, but in life's closing moments the words "He died peacefully" have real significance.

G. K. Chesterton said, "The Lord of compassion seems to pity people for living, rather than for dying." Isn't it true that many of the experiences in life we fear because of the anticipation, but when we actually encounter them they lose much of their terror? I have watched people become physically pale and weak at the thought of speaking before a group. Then, after their initial fright, the feeling of having conquered that fear is exhilarating. I suspect death is like that. Its power to terrorize fades as we near the actual moment of passing.

Attitudes toward Death: The World and the Cults

One of the most common attitudes toward death is denial, which says, "I don't want to think about it." The attitude is not necessarily bad, unless it means we never come around to facing the facts. It is certainly not my intention to have my daily thoughts caught up in the subject of death. In some cases doctors have said that death denial may be therapeutic. An attitude of "I'm not going to die!" may be an affirmation which prolongs life.

Another approach to death is to laugh. Some of the most soft-hearted people are the ones who say, "I'm too mean to die." Humor becomes the protective mechanism that allows us to laugh at ourselves and defy the specter of death. We can hide the fear with a chuckle, which may not always be such a bad idea!

Then there is irrational fear. It can take the form of anxiety that cripples our spirit of daring, or develops into an emotional illness, or phobia, very much like the fear of high places, or crowds, or travel. "Necrophobia," the pathological fear of death, is a fear that stifles ambition and can smother spouse and children through overprotectiveness. It was this sort of intense fear that the writer to the Hebrews addressed when he told how Christ, through His death on the cross, broke the power of the devil to "free those who all their lives were held in slavery by their fear of death" (Hebrews 2:15). The man or woman without Christ can become a slave to fear.

Another common attitude toward death is that it is like a bridge. The principle is that death is a transitional state, a state best seen in the idea of some cults that death is a transition into a happy, bright spirit world of souls who have "crossed over" to a "cosmic" eternity. Spiritism, Eastern mysticism, reincarnation, and countless other occult beliefs offer seductive answers which remove the fear of death but at the expense of denying God's truth.

It is not my purpose in this book to discuss the various beliefs of the cults in detail, or the dangers of believing in a "mystical transition" into another existence, or another life. I want to show that there is a better, surer way to life after death, and that is God's way. Without that assurance, you will never have permanent peace in your life. The cults offer seductive answers that are not grounded in truth. Some are so ludicrous that we wonder how any rational person can believe them.

Dr. Sheldon B. Zablow, a San Diego psychiatrist who treats former cult members, said there are over 2,500 cults operating in the United States. He said that some people do see improvement in their lives for a brief time after entering a cult. "They sometimes give up drugs and alcohol but sacrifice the ability to think and reason. The group becomes the focus of their entire lives. The most disturbing thing is, these are people with serious emotional problems."[4]

A story in a West Coast newspaper told of a cult that has thousands of devotees who believe in reincarnation. Its founder believes she is Mary Magdalene and claims to have lived former lives as Bathsheba, Mona Lisa, and Maria Theresa of Austria. If people can believe they will return as another person, then their responsibility for this life is no longer so important. After all, they believe, we get another chance . . . and another, and another.

It becomes increasingly evident that the way we view death determines, to a surprising degree, the way we live our lives.

Is Fear Unreasonable?

I once heard a man describe his life on a sheep ranch in New Zealand. As he told about the unusual stupidity of sheep, I could see how the frequent references to sheep in the Bible really do apply to us. We follow the crowd. We are helpless when we are attacked, especially if we are attacked by fear. No wonder Christ, the Good Shepherd, continues to assure us, "Fear not, little flock." It may not be a flattering picture, but without His guidance we "baa baa" and wander aimlessly through life, searching for green pastures and stumbling over rocks. "For you were like sheep going astray, but now you have returned to the Shepherd and Overseer of your souls" (1 Peter 2:25).

In the great classic, *Pilgrim's Progress,* Mr. Honest is asked by Mr. Great-heart about one of the Pilgrims. "Did you know Mr. Fearing, who came on the pilgrimage?" Mr. Great-heart asks. Honest replies, "Yes, very well. He was one of the most troublesome pilgrims that I ever met in all my days."

Granted, Mr. Fearing is, as John Bunyan described him, "a troublesome man." But there is something of Mr. Fearing in all of us. Fear is a very painful emotion, one which may immobilize us or cause more pain than a physical blow.

The greatest fear comes when God is a stranger—when our voices and hearts cry out, "God, help me," but our words are muffled because we do not know Him. What do sheep do without a shepherd? They stumble in the darkness. The Bible says, "We all, like sheep, have gone astray, each of us has turned to his own way" (Isaiah 53:6). And that's our picture: going in all directions, bumping into each other, and not being able to find our way home. Fear stalks our every turn.

Reflecting on his years as a pastor, the Rev. Jack Black once told me, "My ministry was filled with persons who feared death; not a natural fear but an anxious fear almost becoming hysterical. Inevitably those persons so described had little or no religious identification, had no close family, had massive egos but low self-esteem, and were bored with life. Compare this human tragedy to the passing of a poor soul, leaving this world surrounded by family and loved ones. Our culture trains us to prepare for almost everything but death. And I include the churches because I have rarely ever heard any public utterance on the subject."

The Bible refers to fear more than 500 times, generally telling us *not* to be afraid. There are so many "fear nots" that we could probably have one for every day in the year—and then some! Look at a few of them:

"Fear none of those things" (Revelation 2:10 KJV).
"Fear not, for I am with thee" (Genesis 26:24 KJV).
"Fear ye not, stand still, and see the salvation of the Lord"
    (Exodus 14:13 KJV).

"Fear not [your enemies]" (Deuteronomy 3:2, 22 KJV).
"Fear not them which kill the body" (Matthew 10:28 KJV).
"Fear not: believe only" (Luke 8:50 KJV).
"Fear not; I am the first and the last" (Revelation 1:17 KJV).

But wait. What do we do with the "fear of the Lord"? If the Bible says "fear not," and yet it also says "fear," which does it mean? The answer is: both. Fear is a two-fold word. It refers to an emotion marked by dread and anxious concern. But it is also the word that means awe and profound reverence. This is the fear that inspires trust and confidence.

When we fear God, we don't cringe before Him like a prisoner robbed of his freedom by a ruthless dictator. Our fear is a love which causes us to treat Him with respect. This is what the prophet Isaiah meant when he said, "The fear of the Lord is the key to this treasure" (Isaiah 33:6). It is a reverence that comes when we see the majesty and holiness of our loving heavenly Father.

There is no shame in being afraid; we're all afraid from time to time. But there's an interesting paradox here, in that if we fear God with all our hearts, there will be nothing else to fear. When I see a child placing his little hand confidently in the bigger hand of his father, I recognize the sort of fear that fosters trust.

When it rains and then freezes over in our mountains in North Carolina, the winding roads become treacherous. I can remember walking with my children, slipping and sliding through the woods. When they held my hand, the children were less afraid. It was up to me not to let them fall down. Our heavenly Father asks us to place our trust in Him and He will steady us.

Was Jesus Afraid?

We know that Jesus was the only person in history who was born without sin, who lived without sin, and who died sinless. Since that is so, why did He display such anguish, sorrow, and fear in the Garden of Gethsemane? There are few episodes in the history of man more dramatic than what took place in that little garden during Christ's final hours on earth.

It might help to imagine ourselves there and try to understand the overwhelming emotion He must have experienced.

Gethsemane means "oil press." Most of us are familiar with olive oil as an ingredient in salads or cooking. In Palestine it was, and is, a valued staple. The Mount of Olives is frequently mentioned in the New Testament and is intimately connected with the devotional life of Jesus. It was on the Mount of Olives that He often sat with His disciples, telling them of events yet to come. And it was to the Mount of Olives that He retired each evening for prayer and rest, after the weary work of the day.

The oldest olive trees in Palestine today are those which are enclosed in the Garden of Gethsemane. Visitors to Jerusalem today can look at them, but they can't get close enough to touch them. Too many curious people have tried to deface those ancient, gnarled trees as they sought a special souvenir from the Holy Land.

When olives are harvested, they are squeezed, pressed, and pulverized under an enormous revolving stone which mashes the fruit to pulp and recovers the valuable oil. It was in the Garden of Gethsemane that the wheel of humiliation, defeat, and eventually death would grind Jesus to the point of His greatest personal agony. Emotional torment is many times more difficult to bear than physical torment. At Gethsemane, the place of the press, the mental anguish was so intense that Jesus pleaded with His Holy Father for release. But only if it was the Father's will.

How we need friends in time of testing! Jesus demonstrated His humanity when He asked His disciples to stay with Him. He wanted and needed them in His time of greatest trial. "My soul is overwhelmed with sorrow, to the point of death; stay here and keep watch with me" (Matthew 26:38). Jesus moved a short distance from His friends, the ones who confidently said they would follow Him, the ones who said they would never deny Him, and He fell on the ground to pray. It couldn't have been too long before His heavy-lidded friends dozed off. The sleepy disciples who had said they would do anything for Him couldn't even sit up and console Him.

As Jesus prayed, His agony was great, "and being in anguish, he prayed more earnestly, and his sweat was like drops of blood falling to the ground" (Luke 22:44). Does that seem impossible? Medical dictionaries describe this condition as "chromidrosis," a state in which intense emotional stress may actually cause the blood vessels to expand so much that they break where they come in contact with the sweat glands. Personally, I cannot begin to comprehend such overpowering emotion.

Jesus prayed three times, "My Father, if it is possible, may this cup be taken from me. Yet not as I will, but as you will" (Matthew 26:39).

Was there a way out? Could Jesus be delivered from the horrors of such a death—at least for a time?

Jesus did not take delight in His approaching crucifixion; He loved life on this earth. He enjoyed the pleasures of walking with His disciples, holding children on His knees, attending a wedding, eating with friends, riding in a boat, or working in the temple at Passover time. To Jesus, death was the enemy. When He prayed, "if it is possible," He wanted to confirm once again if His imminent death were truly the Father's will. Was there some other way?

But what did He mean by His plea to "let this cup pass from me"?

In the Scriptures, "cup" is used figuratively to describe either God's blessing (Psalm 23:5) or God's wrath (Psalm 75:8). Since Jesus would not have prayed for God's blessing to be taken from Him, it is obvious that His use of "cup" here speaks of the divine wrath that Christ would suffer at the Cross as He bore the sins of mankind upon Himself.

How unthinkable it seems to us for Jesus, who knew no sin, to have to bear the sin and guilt of all men. "God made him who had no sin to be sin for us" (2 Corinthians 5:21). Was there no other way of accomplishing the will of the Father without drinking that cup of wrath?

This was the question Jesus was asking—and in complete obedience to the Father's sovereign will Jesus voluntarily accepted the answer. No, there was no other way for a just and loving God to deal with our sins.

Sin must be punished; if God were simply to forgive our sins without judging them, then there would be no justice, no accountability for wrongdoing, and God is not truly holy and just. And if God were simply to judge us for our sins as we deserve to be judged, then there would be no hope of eternal life and salvation for any of us—

for "all have sinned and fall short of the glory of God" (Romans 3:23). His love would have failed to provide a way for our salvation.

The cross was the only way to resolve this awesome dilemma. The conflict of the ages was about to reach its climax. On one hand, our sins were about to be placed on Christ, the sinless One. He would be "clothed" in our sins like a filthy, tattered old garment, and on the cross those sins would be judged—your sins, my sins. He would be the final atoning sacrifice for sin. On the other hand, however, Christ's perfect righteousness would be given to us, like a spotless, gleaming set of new clothes. Sin was therefore judged, and God's justice was satisfied. The door of forgiveness and salvation was opened, and God's love was satisfied. "God made him who had no sin to be sin for us, so that in him we might become the righteousness of God" (2 Corinthians 5:21).

Even as Jesus, in His humanity, struggled within Himself over this awesome predicament, He finally prayed, "Thy will be done." This was not a prayer spoken with a sigh of resignation, but with a strong voice of complete trust. Jesus knew this meant total and absolute surrender to the will of the Father and to the needs of others. Yet, there is a mystery here that we cannot fully understand. Jesus surely experienced the overwhelming awareness of His inevitable sacrifice for the sins of the world. He knew this was His primary mission on earth, for He had said, "For even the Son of Man did not come to be served, but to serve, and to give his life as a ransom for many" (Mark 10:45).

The Garden of Gethsemane is the place where Jesus was revealed to be a true man. He was face to face with the choice between obedience or disobedience. He was not a robot programmed to obey God automatically. He can sympathize with our weaknesses, "For we do not have a high priest who is unable to sympathize with our weaknesses, but we have one who has been tempted in every way, just as we are—yet was without sin" (Hebrews 4:15). Satan tempted Jesus all through His ministry, but the temptations in the wilderness at the beginning of His ministry can scarcely compare to those in the garden. After three years of selfless giving and the stress of that final week, Jesus was never more vulnerable than at this moment of time.

Some skeptics have said that Jesus' suffering in Gethsemane was a sign of weakness. They point out that many martyrs, for instance, died without the intense emotional wrestling of Jesus.

But it is one thing to die for a cause, or to die for country or for another person. It is quite another to die for an entire world, all the accumulated sins of generations past and generations to come. Jesus was to become guilty of murder, adultery, cheating, lying, and all other evil human behavior. It's more than our finite minds can ever comprehend.

One critic of the faith said to a college audience, "Look at Socrates. He didn't anguish over his impending death. He stoically took the hemlock. He proudly held his head high to the end."

Socrates, a great teacher-philosopher of ancient Greece, willingly accepted the death penalty in order to remain true to his convictions. But he died only for himself. No other death in the history of mankind can be compared to the death of Jesus Christ. Many may have suffered as much or more physically, but no one suffered more spiritually. His battle against the powers of darkness, in its essence, meant the triumph of God over Satan. No mere man could defeat Satan—only the God-man, Jesus Christ.

Jesus' Choice: Our Choice

Socrates said, "I go to die, you remain to live. God alone knows which of us goes the better way." As I compare the differences between the deaths of Socrates and Christ, I am struck by a curious contrast. Socrates died by suicide; Jesus by crucifixion. The death of Socrates saved no one, not even himself. Christ's death can save everyone who believes in Him. You and I must also choose between crucifixion and suicide. God has given each of us one life and one time to die. We may live for others or perish in our own selfishness.

If the thought of dying for others is startling, think of what it means to say "Yes" to Jesus, just as He said "Yes" to the Father. When we accept Christ as our Savior and know that He died on the cross for our sins, we have been crucified with Him. Our sins hung on that cross, just as our Lord did.

A friend of mine walks every morning and has been memorizing Bible verses as he walks. He told me that one morning he began to repeat the following verse, and for the first time understood what it meant to be crucified. Here is that verse:

"I am crucified with Christ: nevertheless I live; yet not I, but Christ liveth in me: and the life which I now live in the flesh I live by the faith of the Son of God, who loved me, and gave himself for me" (Galatians 2:20 KJV).

What is the alternative? Instead of Christ living in us, it would be self. To die without Christ is to take one's own life.

Jesus had a choice, and so do we. Did He have fear? Was the "King of Terrors" with Him in that grove of olive trees, stalking Him as He prayed on the damp ground, His sweat mixed with blood? How can we contemplate such intense suffering?

But He has taken away the fear of death for those who trust in Him. We do not need to be ashamed of our fear, but we can rest assured that He will give us strength when we have none of our own, courage when we are cowardly, and comfort when we are hurting.

When fear enters one's life, which it will, the faith which God supplies will defeat the terror and give us victory. Just as knowledge is one of the greatest deterrents to fear, so will our understanding of death enable us to combat fear. The key to victory is found in Solomon's words, "The fear of the Lord is the beginning of knowledge" (Proverbs 1:7).

We fear the unknown, but we can explore that together while we are still in the land of the living.

4

WHY DO SOME

DIE SO SOON?

"We don't own our children. God has given them to us in trust, and normally we spend eighteen to twenty years providing for their training, which represents the period of time we have to fulfill that trust. . . . However, God may transfer our children to His home at any time."

Precious in the sight of the Lord is the death of his saints

Psalm 116:15

My heart aches for the people who suffer when a child, a young person, or a loved one in the prime of life is snatched away by death. I have tried to comfort grieving members of my family or associates and friends who have experienced tragic loss. We expect the old to die, but death seems to be a cruel thief when it steals the young. Carl Jung said, it is "a period placed before the end of the sentence."

A young man whose best friend was killed in a plane crash began a poem with these words, "It is hard to contain so great an emptiness." Those words could be echoed by many throughout the ages.

There are no easy replies to the question of why some die an untimely death, but the Bible does provide us some answers. If we could not find in the Bible solutions to the most difficult questions of life, there would be little worth to this Book.

And the Bible's answers do make a difference in the lives of those confronted with the tragedy of life cut short. In this chapter I have also tried to gather some of the most meaningful stories of those who have had firsthand experience. Out of their suffering we can discover some of the answers they have found.

Ruth's Little Brother

People keep what is precious to them. My wife has a letter written by her father in 1925 that has been a source of comfort to her for many years. Dr. Bell was a medical missionary in China, where he and another doctor helped build and develop a hospital despite civil wars, bandits, and Japanese occupation. Ruth was born in North China, and it was from there her father wrote this important letter.

How amazing it is to discover that the small things we do in our lifetime may be the very touch someone needs in generations to come. Ruth and I believe her father and mother would have wanted this intimate letter to be shared with you.

Little Nelson Bell, Jr., died at the age of ten months, after an illness of just eighteen days. Dr. Bell wrote:

> Virginia and I realized that he was going and we were with him alone when the end came. It was so sweet and so peaceful, no struggle and no evidence of pain, just quietly leaving us and going back to Him.
>
> His going has left an ache in our hearts and our arms

feel very empty, but oh the joy of knowing he is safe. It has but drawn us closer to Him and given us a new tie and joy to look forward to in Heaven. We would not have him back for we know it was His will that he should go. There is no repining, wishing we had used other medicines, etc. We feel that everything that could have possibly been done was done. We had the joy of caring for him ourselves while he was sick and the memory is very sweet. He had been such a perfectly healthy baby, in some ways one of the best developed children I have ever seen and so full of life that he was a favorite with the foreigners and Chinese alike.

Virginia and I had the privilege of fixing him ourselves when he died and then Virginia immediately went to the Talbots where Rosa and Ruth were at school. She wanted to tell them herself, rather than have them hear the news thru the Chinese. They were nearly heartbroken, but it was a wonderful opportunity to bring the great hope that is ours very close and plain to them.

We laid him to rest just at sunset and the service was such a sweet one and we pray was a blessing to the large number of Chinese friends who came. Virginia expressed my feelings exactly as we were leaving the little cemetery (owned by our hospital) when she said, "I have a song in my heart, but it is hard to keep the tears from my eyes." At the grave we sang "Praise God from Whom All Blessings Flow" for this had made the wonderful hope of eternity doubly precious to us. Were it not for that hope we would not be here in China.

A child is born, he may live for a short time, and then die. What good can possibly come from a short life which never was allowed to bloom, from a mind which was never permitted to learn, from a body which was placed in a grave before it had time to grow? I believe God wants us to ask questions, for only then can we find answers. The *Living Bible* says, "Yes, if you want better insight and discernment, and are searching for them as you would for lost money or hidden treasure, then wisdom will be given you, and knowledge of God himself; you will soon learn the importance of reverence for the Lord and of trusting him" (Proverbs 2:3–5).

Trusting Him in life and, yes, in death.

Like a Vapor

Our afflictions would trouble us much less if we knew God's reason for sending them. This is not always the case, however. Sometimes we will never understand during our lifetime why God permits some things to happen. But sometimes we are given precise answers to the meaning of a personal tragedy.

The following story is about friends of mine who discovered, after the sudden death of their eighteen-year-old son, how God can work all things together for good.

The Bible says, "Why, you do not even know what will happen tomorrow. What is your life? You are a mist that appears for a little while and then vanishes" (James 4:14).

Kent left home one afternoon to take his buddy for a flight in his new airplane. He never returned. His plane crashed on takeoff, and two young lives were instantly cut short. Kent was about to enter college to study aeronautical engineering, and he had aspirations of becoming a pilot with Missionary Aviation Fellowship. His parents told me that he accepted Christ as his Savior at our Los

Angeles crusade in 1963. He was then nine years old, and when he was eighteen he went to be with the Lord he loved.

However, in those nine short years this young man had matured in his Christian life more than many others do in a far longer lifetime. He wrote a theme paper in his senior year in high school which showed that he had a clear understanding of what it meant to be a Christian.

In that school assignment he recounted how he had gone to the crusade and become convicted that "this spiritual element was absent in my life because of what the Bible calls sin . . . . It was at this point in Graham's talk that I decided to acknowledge what Christ had done for me by dying on the cross. I asked Him through prayer to make my life what He would have it . . . ."

Yes, Kent's life was cut short before he had fulfilled any of his greater ambitions. But had God answered his prayer to make his life "what He would have it"? His family and friends, in the years that followed that fatal crash, have seen some of the results. Many of his friends, captured by the realization of the uncertainties of life, dedicated themselves to God. One prominent doctor who attended the memorial services was so convicted that his entire life was changed. He later founded a worldwide association of Christian doctors.

Kent's parents went on to develop a ministry to those whose children were suddenly taken by accident or disease.

Clearly, God can turn tragedy into triumph.

When death comes swiftly, especially to a child, the shock can be overwhelming. Without the comfort only God can provide, it is quite difficult to console the stricken loved ones. One woman wrote about finding her six-year-old son crushed beneath a pile of logs behind a sawmill. She said, "Being a nurse, I knew immediately that he was critically injured. I asked the country doctor, who had been summoned from a nearby camp, if we shouldn't get him to a hospital. Standing up, and speaking with a slow Vermont accent, he replied, 'A hospital's not going to do him any good—might better take him to a morgue.' It was then that I realized as I knelt beside his broken, bleeding body, that Craig had gone Home.

"I looked up at the friends and folk who had gathered around and said, 'Do you know where Craig is now? He's up in Heaven with the Lord. He took the Lord as his Savior last spring, and I know he's safe in the arms of Jesus.'

"Humanly speaking, I would have been down hysterically beating the ground and sobbing my heart out, but the Lord gave me peace and strength when I needed it most. Through every minute of the days that followed, my husband and I felt His presence continuously. 'Underneath are the everlasting arms'" (Deuteronomy 33:27).[1]

I had a handsome, bright young nephew by the name of Sandy, the son of Leighton and Jean Ford. An outstanding and fiercely competitive athlete, he almost collapsed at the end of a race his senior year in high school; the newspapers had a picture of him stumbling and falling across the finish line to beat the competition. Upon examination it was discovered he had a rare heart condition which caused his heart to beat far too fast on occasion. Determined not to let it handicap him, Sandy went on to the University of North Carolina. There he became a campus leader and president of the InterVarsity Christian Fellowship, and touched many lives for Christ through his witness. But the old problem with his heart erupted, and after much discussion and prayer the decision was made to operate.

I will never forget visiting him in the hospital on Sunday afternoon on my way from New York to my home in Montreat, North Carolina. My sister Jean came in, as well as Sandy's girl friend, and we had a wonderful time of talking, praying, and laughing. Later I went to Winston-Salem to visit his father Leighton, who was holding a week of meetings in a church there, and we prayed and committed Sandy to the Lord. On Thursday the doctors operated, and everyone was optimistic that his problem would be solved. But they could not get his heart started again. Sandy's vibrant young life, so full of promise and potential and dedication to Christ, had come to an end.

Our family could not help but wonder "Why?" How could we reconcile Sandy's death with the purposes of a loving God? Ultimately we had to confess that we did not know the full answer—but God did, and He could be trusted. My wife Ruth came up with the best answer, however, by pointing out that the work God had given to Sandy was completed. Since that time a book about his life and death has become a best seller, inspiring and challenging thousands. A fund set up in his memory provides scholarships for dozens of students each year who are preparing for careers in missions and evangelism. God has used Sandy's death to touch lives in a way no one could ever have envisioned.

As I said at the memorial service for my nephew, Sandy, "His life was not cut short, it was completed."

The late Joe Bayly wrote about the death of the young from firsthand experience. He lost three children: one at eighteen days, after surgery; another at five years, with leukemia; the third at eighteen years, after a sledding accident complicated by mild hemophilia. Joe said, "Of all deaths, that of a child is most unnatural and hardest to bear." He did not underestimate the grief of parents. He added, "When a child dies, part of the parents is buried."

For others to assess "the peace of God, which transcends all understanding" (Philippians 4:7) as being an attitude of indifference or callousness is a mistake. Intense emotions well up in the hearts and minds of those who suffer the loss of a child or a young person. But the Christian does have the sure promise from Jesus that "I will not leave you comfortless: I will come to you" (John 14:18 KJV).

"You cannot imagine what it is like to live with a dying child," a mother told us. Faith is tested to a degree that those of us who have never experienced such a trial cannot imagine.

Joe Bayly, who knew that testing, said, "To spoil a child at a time of serious illness is to do him no favor. Few things are more liable to give away the fact that we are uptight about him than special treatment to a child. This is the time for treatment as usual, including—hard as it may be—necessary discipline. Of course we will spend more time with the sick child."[2]

Erika's Story

Erika was Lauren and Dave's first baby. She was the picture of a beautiful child, welcomed by the congregation of the church where Dave was youth pastor. After a few months a concern began to grow because little Erika had trouble holding her head up. She was unable to control her arms, and her other physical skills were not improving. At one year of age, it was obvious that she hadn't grown as she should. Her worried young parents took her to medical specialists and neurologists for diagnosis. The consensus was that she had a rare disease for which there was no known cure.

During her second year Erika was susceptible to any illness that came her way. She had pneumonia several times and was in and out of hospitals. Lauren began to stay away from church activities, gave up her Bible study group, and devoted all her time to caring for Erika. She thought if she guarded the child from possible infection she might get stronger.

Erika's battle for life was frustrating for Lauren and Dave, because there didn't seem to be anything the medical profession could do for her. Lauren recalled how she reached one of her lowest emotional points when someone thoughtlessly said to her, "It is because of your lack of faith that Erika isn't being healed."

Early one morning Dave went to check on his little girl. He noticed that her skin was a brownish gray rather than her normal pink tone, and her doctor advised him to rush Erika to the hospital emergency room. By the time they arrived she had gone into shock, and immediate attempts were made to resuscitate her. The chances for her survival were slim. However, she was revived, and when they heard she was improving Dave said, "The time was not ripe for God to take her home. Thankful, we were trusting His care and His timing."

Lauren was pregnant with their second child, and as the nature of Erika's illness became known to the staff doctors at the hospital, that unborn child became the object of increasing concern. A genetics specialist told

Lauren and Dave that any of their future children would have a one in four chance of being born with the same disease.

One day when Dave was out of the hospital, Erika's doctor suggested to Lauren that she should think about having an abortion. "At least consider amniocentesis to know whether you want to terminate this pregnancy," he said.

Dave was angry when he heard that abortion had been recommended. "That suggestion is from the pit!" he wrote in his diary. "What else can be expected from someone with no spiritual receiver?"

During the next two weeks the young couple experienced a roller coaster of emotions. One day Dave wrote, "Overall we are very encouraged and feel that perhaps Erika still has a fighting chance." But within a couple of days, he and Lauren were asked the big question: what measures should be taken to resuscitate Erika if a seizure sends her into failure? "This is agony," wrote Dave. "How can we be involved in making such choices? We are praying that we will have God's supernatural wisdom regarding this trial. Nothing else can possibly suffice."

The doctor who had suggested the abortion told Dave and Lauren that their stability helped him do his job. But he wondered if they were suppressing their feelings and would suffer later as a result. "We admitted openly," Dave said, "that we cry together and hurt together when we are alone . . . sometimes with others, too. But we know a real peace in believing that God is sovereignly controlling this situation."

On the last day of little Erika's earthly life, her parents were faced with major decisions that had to be made immediately. The doctors asked if they wanted them to employ extraordinary measures to keep Erika alive. Her parents decided it was time to say "no." As Lauren held Erika in her arms and softly sang to her, they watched their child's life slip away.

Erika touched lives because of her mother and father, because of the friends who visited the hospital and the churches that prayed. And Lauren and Dave have had two more healthy little daughters since Erika died. What if they had listened to medical advice to abort?

Erika's story is not a closed chapter. Her parents saw that many witnessed about God with new boldness during the time Erika was in the hospital. Lauren said, "Time doesn't heal . . . it's what you do with the time that heals." As Jack Black has said, "A long life or a short life are of equal importance to God."

Robin's Story

Millions of people throughout the world have been touched in the past thirty years by the life of a little girl who lived two short years. Her name was Robin and she was born with borderline Down's syndrome. She also suffered from a heart condition that gave her a very small chance of surviving for long.

One day Robin's mother received a phone call from a minister she had never met. He said to her, "You and your husband will soon begin to receive what our Lord wants you to learn from this child. In my opinion these little children are allowed to come into this world to bless lives. Their presence teaches patience and understanding that makes those around them more godly. Mrs. Rogers, you are truly blessed by the Lord, and you may be sure that your sweet Robin will one day be rewarded handsomely in the hereafter."[3]

Robin's parents are my long-time friends, Roy

Rogers and Dale Evans, and the book Dale wrote, *Angel Unaware,* became a bestseller. Dale told of the agonizing visits to doctors, only to be told there was no hope. She told of the heart-wrenching feelings of watching a helpless child suffer.

When Dale wrote that amazing little book, it wasn't from her own viewpoint, but as if the baby, Robin, were speaking from heaven. Robin talked about her Daddy, and how seeing crippled children always hurt him and caused him to question why a loving God would allow children to suffer. And so Roy began to read his Bible, "as though he had never seen it before." From the experience of having an exceptional child, a new Roy Rogers was born.

Dale has said that she is grateful that the Lord sent Robin to them, for it made her walk closer to God.

It has not been an easy time for Roy and Dale: two other children died at an early age. But through the lessons they have learned, the good they have done for other sufferers, and their sincere commitment to the Lord, they're able to sing "Peace in the Valley" from the heart.

The Guilt Syndrome

Often when a child is suffering, parents will ask themselves, "What did I do wrong? How did I sin?" Guilt begins to accentuate the pain. Sometimes guilt comes in the guise of, "If only I had . . . ." and then they review again and again all of the things they think might have been done to avoid the illness or the accident. I was told of one woman who spent years blaming herself because she had taken her little daughter to a park and allowed her to play in a stream. The child caught a cold which developed into a fatal bout with pneumonia. The mother allowed her own sense of blame and guilt to plague her for the rest of her life.

Even the disciples asked Jesus, "Who sinned, this man or his parents, that he was born blind?" (John 9:2). They, too, thought that affliction was something always brought about by sin.

Granted, there are diseases and deaths that are the direct result of man's sin. We are surrounded by these every day. However, in the example of the blind man, and in the case of innocent children, Jesus had the answer. He said, "Neither this man nor his parents sinned . . . but this happened so that the work of God might be displayed in his life" (John 9:3).

I don't mean that parents of children who are born with an affliction, or become ill, or have an accident and die, are not sinners. We all are. However, if we believe that God punishes our children or loved ones because we have sinned, we have fallen into a cruel fallacy. Blaming ourselves leads to depression and unjustified guilt, and blaming a husband or wife may cause a breakdown in a marriage at a time when a sick child or other children desperately need the security of the family.

It may shock some parents to learn that we don't own our children. God has given them to us in trust, and normally we spend eighteen to twenty years providing for their training, which represents the period of time we have to fulfill that trust. (Don't misunderstand me— we don't cut them off at that point. Even when they are adults, they are our children. Relationships don't change, only obligations.)

However, God may transfer our children to His

home at any time. If Jesus were to come today and say, "I want to take over all the teaching and training of your little boy," you would gladly let go of his hand and place it in the hand of Jesus, wouldn't you? That is what happens when He takes a child to heaven.

Why "Suffer Little Children"?

Jesus' disciples were irritated. The Master was tired from teaching all day, and here were all of these little kids pushing Him around. Can't you imagine the scene? Their mothers wanted the boys and girls to touch Him, and the disciples sought to shoo the children away. But Jesus reached out and said, "Suffer little children, and forbid them not, to come unto me; for of such is the kingdom of heaven" (Matthew 19:14 KJV).

Translated into modern vernacular, that meant, "Let the children alone, don't stop them from coming to Me. Don't you know that the kingdom of heaven belongs to children?"

We must all enter the kingdom of heaven with the simple faith and trust of a child, but a special place is reserved in the heart of the Lord for the young ones.

One mother of a child who died said, "I thank God for loaning us the little fellow for a few years, and for the knowledge that we will see him again when we are united with Christ after death. What a joyous reunion. What a wonderful Savior, to provide the gift of eternal life!"

How true it is that the Lord must love little children, because He calls so many of them home. Our hope that those who die as children are lovingly taken by God to heaven was expressed beautifully by King David when

82

his infant son died: "I will go to him, but he will not return to me" (2 Samuel 12:23).

"If I Should Die before I Wake"

When children mumble that little prayer, I doubt if most of them think much about it. "I pray the Lord my soul to take," is the way it ends. Today that prayer has been neglected by most modern parents, and even banned by some. But what do we tell our children about death?

When I was growing up on a farm, death was an ever-present reality. The animals gave birth and some died. Death was not a secret. My children were reared with a menagerie of pets. Inevitably, some of them died. Somehow, without a long, psychological explanation, our kids became aware that death is part of the human experience and can be expected.

Our daughter Anne Lotz is one of the great Bible teachers in the country today. But I can remember she had a wonderful police dog when she was about thirteen years of age. The dog died. Anne of course was in tears. How she loved that dog. I remember taking her into my study and explaining to her that God was training her and teaching her for events that might happen in her life to come, and this would make her depend upon the Lord far more. We got down and prayed. And I remember that extra-special little time with Anne, never dreaming what she was to become as her life was strengthened by such events and the study of Scripture.

In fact, pets are a very good way of teaching children about death. The death of a pet may be a child's dress rehearsal for other losses. If we treat that death with respect and dignity, answering the child's questions, we will probably help prepare him for the inevitable encounters with the death of a friend or relative. Of course, the death of a person is a very different matter: friends and loved ones are not so easily replaced.

When a child has a pet that dies, the wise parent sometimes goes out and gets a new puppy or kitten to replace the beloved pet. The child is not given the chance to grieve too long and unnecessarily. A wonderful, faithful pet becomes part of a family, and when it is gone, it is sure to be missed. But given time, a new pet can bring his own special love into a child's life.

When Ruth was a child in China she had a mongrel dog named Tar Baby. When he died, he was buried beside a wall in the compound. In 1980 when she returned to her birthplace with her brother, Clayton, and two sisters, Rosa and Virginia, one of the first things she did was look for Tar Baby's grave. Fifty years later she remembered where that little dog's grave was.

Whenever a child encounters death, it is important that he or she be able to talk about it. I am concerned when the members of a family keep their feelings to themselves. When our children were growing up, I was not always around to share all of their daily challenges (though I was there more than most people think). But they all tell how their Mom would be available to listen to their problems, and if she wasn't around, her parents, Dr. and Mrs. Bell, were.

To tell children about the death of someone they love may be one of the most difficult tasks of life. But even well-intentioned misinformation can do more damage than the blunt truth.

Seven-year-old John was told that his uncle had gone to sleep. For many nights, John refused to go to sleep, afraid of what lurked in the darkness of his room. It took months for that little boy to return to his natural sleeping habits.

It is equally cruel to tell a child that the dead person has taken a trip. Death is not a trip, but a destination. Taking a trip implies that the person who died abandoned his loved ones without a good-bye, and it holds out the false hope that he may be returning.

Christians must be careful to tell a child about death without making God sound cruel. "God took Aunt Betsy" may cause a child to ask, "What kind of a God would take someone away like that?" When I told my nephew Kevin that his brother, Sandy, had died, I remember saying, "Sandy is in heaven."

The best thing we can do for a child is tell him about death without hiding facts. Visualizing heaven will give comfort, and describing a place where there is no more suffering or problems is something even the smallest child can understand. We shouldn't be afraid to talk openly about the person who has died, especially recalling good times or funny stories about them.

The Facts of Death

Kids tend to think of death as a game to play. "Shoot 'em dead!" is not a serious command. Our children played many games of cops and robbers or cowboys and Indians in the hills surrounding our North Carolina home. Today's kids don their camouflage outfits and pocket their Rambo knives for the great "search and destroy."

As they grow older, we talk about teaching "the facts of life." The "facts of death" are natural counterparts. However, in these days of "megadeath," with news of earthquakes in South America, plane crashes in our capital cities, hurricanes on Atlantic beaches, or starvation in Africa, we have been bombarded with images of death to the point of indifference. It is estimated that children may see as many as 15,000 graphic depictions of death before reaching adolescence. Psychologists are saying the increasing violence on television is already having serious consequences in the lives of children as they grow up.

However, newspaper accounts and images on the screen seem remote until someone you know dies. This is when we need to talk, not hide the facts. And how we talk about it is more important than the exact words we say.

After the tragic explosion of the *Challenger* space ship in 1986, the students in Christa McAuliffe's class had a particularly rough time coping with their grief and the reality of their teacher's death. The difficulty of accepting the deaths of the crew members was magnified by the impact of seeing the fateful explosion being replayed over and over on television. Those who watched the news that day will have a hard time forgetting it.

However sad it may be, truth is easier for a child to handle than evasiveness. A Christian needs to deal honestly with a child's questions about birth, the body, and the soul.

A psychologist wrote in the *Los Angeles Times*, "Before an adult can help a child, though, it is necessary for the adult to understand the mourning process, be able to speak about death, face one's own mortality and understand that the most important thing is to be able to feel and express those feelings with tears, words and physical activity as an outlet for anger."[4]

In *Children's Letters to God,* a little boy wrote, "Dear God, What is it like when a person dies? Nobody will tell me. I just want to know, I don't want to do it. Your friend, Mike."[5]

If I could answer Mike, I would first sit down with my arms around him and say, "Mike, everything must die sometime. When someone is dead, the body they have lived in stops breathing and moving, and seeing, and hearing. The person who had that body doesn't hurt or worry any longer. That is his earthly body. But we also have a spirit, Mike, and when we ask Jesus to come into our hearts, we will have a spiritual body from heaven. You see, son, God tells us that we will have new bodies that are strong and healthy, that are supernatural, spiritual bodies."

Losing a Loved One

Mike, and all the children like him, need simple, honest answers and lots of love. If Mike should have someone he loves die, he needs to be able to express himself without being judged for his actions. He may show indifference or anger. He may revert to baby habits.

One friend told me about his eleven-year-old son, who developed a clinging attitude after the death of his big brother. The boy would cry if his parents wanted to go out for the evening. He wouldn't go anywhere without Mom or Dad. He left for a weekend with the Boy Scouts and became sick to his stomach before the troop reached their campsite. Fortunately, an understanding counselor brought him home without forcing him to stay.

Losing a parent through death is experienced by about one in six young people before they reach eighteen, and the statistics today on the number of children of divorce indicate that millions of young people are victims of a loss sometimes worse than death.

One of the burdens on my heart is for the churches to provide the extended arms of love to kids who are victims. A hurting, resentful child will grow into an adult who believes no one cares, and he continues the cycle of pain. Most of all, adults need to recognize that the Bible tells us to care for widows and orphans, "Religion that God our Father accepts as pure and faultless is this: to look after orphans and widows in their distress and to keep oneself from being polluted by the world" (James 1:27), and it is the obligation of the entire Christian community.

Children feel the need to talk about the death of a loved one, just as adults do. Stephen was eleven when his father died. He said in an interview, "I stayed home from school for two weeks and when I went back I wasn't crying anymore. My friends said, 'It doesn't seem like you're very sad your father died. It doesn't seem like you miss him.' I did feel sad, but I just didn't want to cry in front of them, you know. One kid even said, 'You must be glad your father died because you're not crying.' That remark really got me so upset that I told my mom about it when I got home. She said it was because when they saw me, it made them all think how sad they would be if their fathers died and they didn't realize I had done all my crying at home."

Stephen continued, "I don't know if I'll ever see my

father again. No one really knows about heaven because they haven't been dead yet. But I think part of my father is still with me. His body isn't, but his spirit is. If he's anywhere, I guess he's in heaven with my grandfather. At night I usually pray to God and say, 'Please help Dad and Grandpop to have a fun time up there.'"[6]

I would like to tell all the Stephens out there that, yes, there really is a heaven. Jesus came from there and He died and has gone back to prepare a place for us.

What Happens to the Family?

When a child or young person dies, parents sometimes elevate him or her to a pedestal never attained in life. The one who is gone may become the most perfect son or daughter who ever lived, at least in the memory of mother and father. One woman told me of resenting her dead sister all her life, because her mother always talked about "little Lucille" as if she had been a saint.

It is unfair to attribute virtues beyond a person's true character. On the other hand, it can be healing to blot out the bitter memories and grasp the happy ones.

A family either comes closer together as a result of death, or is driven farther apart. Nothing ever seems to remain the same. The death of a child, especially a firstborn or an only child, can place severe strains on a marriage. A psychiatrist said, "No adequate studies have been carried out, but some authorities estimate that as many as 75 percent of couples may separate after the death of a child, especially if they do not seek competent help."[7]

But there is help. C. S. Lewis says, "God whispers to us in our pleasures, speaks in our conscience, but shouts in our pains: it is His megaphone to rouse a deaf world."[8]

No one likes to be shouted at, and yet God loves us so much that when troubles come, He is there to call us closer to Him.

Children may be the little trumpet players who bring us to our senses, and to our knees. "Jesus said, 'Let the little children come to me, and do not hinder them, for the kingdom of heaven belongs to such as these'" (Matthew 19:14).

5

JOURNEY THROUGH

THE VALLEY

"Many people say they do not fear death, but the process of dying. It's not the destination, but the trip that they dread."

Even though I walk through the valley of the shadow of death, I will fear no evil, for you are with me . . . .

Psalm 23:4

Dr. Donald Grey Barnhouse was one of America's great preachers. His first wife died from cancer when she was in her thirties, leaving three children under the age of twelve. Barnhouse chose to preach the funeral sermon himself. What does a father tell his motherless children at a time like that?

On his way to the service, he was driving with his little family when a large truck passed them on the highway, casting a shadow over their car. Barnhouse turned to his oldest daughter who was staring disconsolately out the window, and asked, "Tell me, sweetheart, would you rather be run over by that truck or its shadow?"

The little girl looked curiously at her father and said, "By the shadow, I guess. It can't hurt you."

Dr. Barnhouse said quietly to the three children, "Your mother has not been overrun by death, but by the shadow of death. That is nothing to fear." At the funeral he used the text from the Twenty-third Psalm, which so eloquently expresses this truth. That illustration from Dr. Barnhouse's own experience has been used by countless preachers to help other families face their fear of death.

Many people say they do not fear death, but the *process* of dying. It's not the destination, but the trip that they dread.

John Newton, a one-time slave trader, was converted and became a great preacher and hymn writer in the Church of England. Two years before his death, in 1807, he was so weak that he could hardly stand in his pulpit; someone had to support him as he preached. Shortly before he died, when he was confined to his room and unable to move, he told a friend, "I am like a person going on a journey in a stagecoach, who expects its arrival every hour and is frequently looking out of the window for it . . . . I am packed and sealed, and ready for the post."[1]

You may have heard of Newton; he wrote some words which are sung around the world: "Amazing grace, how sweet the sound."

The Dangers of Denial

Whether our last trip is by stagecoach, slow and arduous, or by jet, swift and smooth, the journey through the valley eventually comes to a stop. How should we travel, and how can we help the ones we love along the way?

As Christians we are constantly bombarded with attitudes and values which are contrary to biblical teaching. Even though the subject of death has come out of the closet, the denial of one's own mortality is instinctive in most of us. No matter how well we take care of ourselves, there may come a time when we face a severe health problem. Sometimes we are not given a choice about our physical or mental condition. How can we live in a basically non-Christian culture and cope with the despair that may come when death seems near?

In her inimitable bravado, Katherine Hepburn said, "I think we're finally at a point where we've learned to see death with a sense of humor. I have to. When you're my age, it's as if you're a car. First a tire blows, and you get that fixed. Then a headlight goes, and you get that fixed. And then one day, you drive into a shop, and the man says, 'Sorry, Miss, they don't have this make anymore.'"[2]

But a time comes when the humor becomes deadly serious. Anyone who is told he has a fatal illness cannot just laugh it off. The first reaction is, "You must be wrong." "Not me." Bad news is all too frequently met, first, with disbelief.

Denial can be very dangerous. A prominent urologist endured severe lower back pains over a long period of time; although he had diagnosed patients with similar conditions, he refused to get treatment until his own condition was beyond hope of a medical cure. He did not want to hear the bad news, so he opted for no news.

Dr. Ruth Kopp, a Christian doctor specializing in clinical oncology, has had many years of experience with terminally ill patients. She wrote: "The first important effect of denial I've seen in my relationships with patients is that it produces a partial deafness. Although the hospital staff told Jesse (the patient) that he had widespread, inoperable cancer, he was deaf to much of what he had heard. He was not unique in that respect!"[3]

A terminally ill patient may reject what he has heard, and then deny the need for treatment. Some will listen to the doctor's diagnosis and then begin a round of searching for other doctors who will give them happier news. Of course, there is nothing wrong with getting other qualified opinions; this should not be considered denial. Others look for unorthodox methods and spend time and money for temporary, often fraudulent, cures for their symptoms instead of facing the reality of their condition.

Denial isn't necessarily a sign of weakness, but a normal emotion that needs to be voiced. Sometimes it can serve as a protective mechanism to shield a person from threatening situations before the individual is emotionally ready to handle them. If we persist in denial, however, we are cutting ourselves off from the help we need—from others and from God.

The prophet Jeremiah said, "You can't heal a wound by saying it's not there" (Jeremiah 6:14 LB). And yet we want to ignore a diagnosis about our physical state if it is unpleasant.

Chaplain Phil Manly tells a story that illustrates the force that denial can play in masking the truth. A badly burned baby was admitted to the USC Medical Center burn ward in Los Angeles. The mother was with the baby when the child died. The next day the nurse on the ward received a call from the mother asking how her baby was and what time she could visit. The nurse and Chaplain Manly were able to bring her lovingly to accept the reality of her baby's death.

Jesus had a difficult time with the attitude of denial in His disciples. He told them repeatedly that He would be betrayed and crucified, but they refused to listen. Peter even rebuked Him for saying that He was going to be killed and after three days rise again: "From that time on Jesus began to explain to his disciples that he must go to Jerusalem and suffer many things at the hands of the elders, chief priests and teachers of the law, and that he must be killed and on the third day be raised to life. Peter took him aside and began to rebuke him. 'Never, Lord!' he said. 'This shall never happen to you!'" (Matthew 16:21, 22).

Peter knew Jesus told the truth, but he did not want to hear it.

When Truth Hurts—or Heals

The Bible tells us to "speak the truth in love," and yet there are times when the truth seems so harsh that we play games. One way to respond when a terminally ill person is in the denial stage is to join him in the ostrich attitude. But Dr. Ruth Kopp warns, "If your response is behavior that is harmful to the individual, it is inappropriate."[4] Most people can't face the fact of their own deaths twenty-four hours a day, and need to pretend, at least for a while, that the situation may be just a bad dream.

We may respond to someone's denial by avoiding it. Many people who have been told they have just a few weeks or months left have lived to laugh at the diagnosis years later. A Christian may have complete confidence that God has healed him or her, despite medical reports to the contrary. A realistic answer, given with gentleness and love, might be, "We know that God can heal, and He does. But we don't know what He has in store for you or for me. Let's trust the doctors for treatment, and continue to pray for healing, asking for God's will." One doctor said he used the "wait and see" response whenever a terminally ill person said that God had healed him or her. If He hasn't, then they will face that reality later.

No One Wins

Some types of denial can be dangerous for the patient and loved ones. I refer specifically to the "Let's Spare Them" game. The patient knows he or she is terminally ill. There are important things such a person wants to say to his wife and children, but he is afraid they cannot accept the fact that he may soon die, so he spares them any painful conversations. His wife, knowing her husband's time is short, wants to keep the atmosphere cheerful, so she doesn't ask the questions she needs to ask about the family and finances that are a burden on her heart. His family would like to tell him some of the things they never got around to saying when he was well, but they're afraid to upset him. Everyone plays the game, and no one is a winner.

What if, instead, dying people were urged to express themselves and talk openly about their illness? And what if the loved ones listened to such concerns, instead of ignoring them? Nothing soothes loneliness or depression as much as being able to talk about those fears and concerns.

Job's Friends: Who Needs Enemies?

Job was afflicted with so many physical and emotional problems that his name is always associated with suffering. His wealth was taken from him and his sons and daughters were crushed when a great wind demolished the house where they were dining. Job was struck with terrible boils from head to foot. His wife and brothers shunned him and children ran from the sight of him. Those who loved him turned against him. He became a joke among the people who had once respected him.

Along came those "well-meaning friends" who tried to explain the cause of his pain. One "friend" told him he was being punished by God less than he deserved. Another argued if he had been pure and good, God would hear his prayers and answer him.

In various modern guises, many of "Job's friends" are still among us today. There is nothing more dangerous than a half-truth, so let's examine what the Bible says about the sickness, disease, and pain which usually precede all but sudden, accidental deaths.

We know that when God created Adam and Eve, they were holy and healthy. They were created in His perfect image and were to remain perfect human specimens. More than that, they were not meant to experience death. But Satan ruined these two divine masterpieces, and as a result of their decision to disobey God, sin, sickness, and death entered paradise. So, human sin was the first cause of sickness and death. Since that moment in the Garden of Eden, pain and death have been the heritage of the entire human race. " . . . sin entered the world through one man, and death through sin, and in this way death came to all men, because all sinned" (Romans 5:12).

Even the strain of Christian service can result in sickness. Daniel was a devoted servant of the Lord, and when he saw a vision of things to come, he fainted and was ill for many days (Daniel 8:26, 27).

The apostle Paul likewise experienced frequent bouts of illness and physical weakness. He recalled to the Corinthians, "I came to you in weakness" (1 Corinthians 2:3). He prayed also that God would take his problem away: ". . . there was given me a thorn in my flesh, a messenger of Satan, to torment me. Three times I pleaded with the Lord to take it away from me. But he said to me, 'My grace is sufficient for you, for my power is made perfect in weakness.' Therefore I will boast all the more gladly about my weaknesses, so that Christ's power may rest on me. That is why, for Christ's sake, I delight in weaknesses, in insults, in hardships, in persecutions, in difficulties. For when I am weak, then I am strong" (2 Corinthians 12:7b–10). I have known many Christian workers who have risked their lives and their health in serving the Lord, although I have known others whose ministries would have lasted longer if they had taken better care of themselves and learned to relax.

A leading cause of sickness today is our high-pressure lifestyle. Heart disease, ulcers, and some types of cancer often may be attributable to our ambitious pursuits and reckless living. We know that neglecting our need for good diet, rest, and mental habits can lead to serious physical problems. The Bible says, "My people are destroyed from lack of knowledge" (Hosea 4:6).

We cannot always know or understand God's purpose in allowing us to endure physical or mental trials. I must admit that when I see someone suffer who has devoted his life to the Lord and has led an exemplary life, I find it difficult to understand. Nevertheless, we know we can trust God and His love, even when we do not understand.

My friend of many years, the late Herbert Lockyer,

in his book, *All the Promises of the Bible,* illuminates some of his discoveries from the Bible concerning the purposes of sickness.[5]

One purpose is to teach us God's laws. The psalmist said, "It was good for me to be afflicted so that I might learn your decrees" (Psalm 119:71).

Another purpose of sickness and suffering is to perfect the person who sins. It's the idea that God will pull us up short to strengthen us for His purpose. "And the God of all grace, who called you to his eternal glory in Christ, after you have suffered a little while, will himself restore you and make you strong, firm and steadfast" (1 Peter 5:10).

Suffering is also meant to prepare us for a coming glory. Peter writes, "Dear friends, do not be surprised at the painful trial you are suffering, as though something strange were happening to you. But rejoice that you participate in the sufferings of Christ, so that you may be overjoyed when his glory is revealed" (1 Peter 4:12, 13).

Also, suffering equips us to comfort others ". . . so that we can comfort those in any trouble with the comfort we ourselves have received from God" (2 Corinthians 1:4).

God doesn't comfort us to make us comfortable, but to make us comforters.

In addition, suffering can give us opportunities to witness. The world is a gigantic hospital; nowhere is there a greater chance to see the peace and joy of the Lord than when the journey through the valley is the darkest.

Gene and Helen Poole were Christians who had been married for sixty-five years. When Helen was in the final weeks of her life, unable to move or speak, it was the witness of her faithful husband, spending all day beside her bed in his wheelchair, that touched the lives of the staff and visitors at the convalescent home.

Perhaps you are going through a period of suffering right now. It may be because of some physical illness which has afflicted you, or it may be because of a broken relationship, a financial difficulty, or some other reason. What is your reaction to it? Are you resentful and bitter, demanding that God change your situation or lashing out at those around you for what you consider unjust treatment? Or have you yielded your life—including your suffering—to Christ and asked Him to work for His glory through your suffering, even if you do not fully understand it?

When the word came of the illness of Lazarus (who would die and then be raised from the dead by Jesus), Jesus declared, "This sickness will not end in death. No, it is for God's glory so that God's Son may be glorified through it" (John 11:4). The same could be said of much of our suffering, as we seek God's will and strength.

The Bible warns that bitterness never solves anything, but only hurts both us and those around us: "See to it . . . that no bitter root grows up to cause trouble and defile many" (Hebrews 12:15). It also promises us that God can bring a harvest of good in our lives through our suffering, if we will let Him. "No discipline seems pleasant at the time, but painful. Later on, however, it produces a harvest of righteousness and peace for those who have been trained by it" (Hebrews 12:11).

William W. Kinsley has written, "Just as soon as we turn toward Him with loving confidence, and say, 'Thy will be done,' whatever chills or cripples or enslaves our spirits, clogs their powers, or hinders their development, melts away in the sunshine of His sympathy. He does not free us from the pain, but from its power."

Yes, God is with us in the midst of our suffering, and He can bless us in ways we could never have imagined. Lay your burden of suffering at the feet of Christ—who suffered on the cross for you—and ask Him to help you not only bear it but experience His victory and peace in the midst of it.

Do We Go through Stages?

Elisabeth Kübler-Ross was one of the first secular psychologists to observe that there are five stages that patients and their loved ones may go through in the dying process. Most people in the medical and psychological fields agree that a person doesn't march through the five stages of denial, anger, bargaining, depression, and acceptance like a programmed robot. These stages may coexist, be reversed, or be skipped, but the pattern is common in many sufferers.

Marian Holten cared for terminally ill patients for more than forty years and had many experiences seeing her patients through the valley. She had been a student nurse in the 1940s when her first assignment was to sit with a dying, comatose patient. She said those were the days when there was more personal than machine care. She pulled up a chair by the bedside, prepared for a long, tedious vigil. Suddenly she was startled when her patient, who had been unable to move or speak for weeks, opened his eyes, sat up in bed and looked around. A beautiful expression came over his face, and then he fell back on his pillow, dead.

From that time on, Marian asked to be assigned to

the terminally ill. She wanted to know more about the dying experience, what happened at the moment of death, and how to help her patients through those final hours.

Denial is so strong that patients will insist they are going to do things they are incapable of doing. Marian told of a young girl who was in the last stages of acute leukemia and kept insisting that she was going to Canada. How do caring people respond when they know the desire cannot be carried out? We do not need to lie, but we must be supportive. Marian taught her student nurses to make a statement which was positive. She would say, "I can see that's something you are happy about. Tell me about Canada. Is it someplace you've always wanted to go?" Taking someone's mind off his or her illness, without supporting his or her denial, is the honest way.

When my mother was in her final days, Rose Adams would get her dressed to go out, even when she knew Mother would not be able to go. It was a game, but it made Mother happy, and that was the most important thing.

Denial through Anger and Indifference

Anger is another very human response from those who are very ill. One patient became so angry that when the nurse came in to take his temperature in the morning, he shouted at her, "Get out of here, I can't stand your face." Marian Holten remembered another time when a patient threw a full urinal at her. How can caring people handle other people's anger? One way is with humor. Later Marian who was on the receiving end of the outburst poked her head cautiously in the door and said, "Hey, is it okay to come in now?" He laughed, realizing how unreasonably hard he had been on her, and soon they were friends.

Another type of denial is to ignore those we think are past understanding. We should never assume that people do not hear what we are saying. Among the "living dead" are those who are very much alive. Nurses report that family members, and even hospital personnel, talk around a comatose patient as if he or she were already dead. At first all the family members come to the bedside of their dying loved one. Then, they begin to return to their other activities and, just when the patient needs them the most, there is no one around. "It's taking him so long to die," someone says in his presence; or, "I just wish the Lord would take him and get it over with."

One nurse told how she talked quietly and encouragingly to her patient all the time she was caring for his needs, even though the doctors said he didn't know anything that was happening. He miraculously came out of his coma and upon hearing the voice of this nurse said, "Oh, you're the one who talked to me."

Denial through Bargaining

Another of the stages is bargaining. A Las Vegas showgirl was admitted to the hospital and it was discovered that she was in the final stages of cancer. A year before she had discovered a lump on her breast, but she chose to ignore the symptoms. Her body was her fortune, and she refused to have it "mutilated," as she described it. When she had to have surgery to save her life she was angry. Soon she thought her beauty was gone, but she still propped herself up in bed and spent hours every day applying make-up. She became garish looking and increasingly bitter. One day a beautiful student nurse came into the room and the showgirl looked at her and remarked to Nurse Nolten, "I would give anything if I could be like . . ." and then she cut off her bargaining plea and ended pathetically, "But I don't have anything left to give, do I?"

Ironically, at that point she was finally past denying and bargaining and at last able to accept her position. It was then she said, "I can't handle this alone."

When we have "nothing left to give," God says, "All I want is you, beloved. Trust Me." The Great Physician is willing and able to take our burdens, if we will just hand them over to Him. Life and death is not a do-it-yourself project.

Divine Healing: Truth and Consequences

When little Erika was on life-support systems, hundreds of people were praying for her healing. Instead, the Lord took Erika to be with Himself. At the same time, in another hospital, Ron Stokes was in intensive care after a severe stroke. Hundreds of people all over the country were praying for Ron. He recovered, and as a result of caring Christian friends, accepted Christ. Why did God cure Ron and not Erika? Were prayers any less fervent or the faith of loved ones any weaker in one case than the other? No, not at all. Does God heal today? Of course He does, but not always. He can heal in response to prayer and faith; He can heal through the skill of physicians or the effectiveness of medicines.

When Ruth's sister, Rosa, was a senior at Wheaton College she collapsed in chapel and was rushed to the hospital. They thought she had appendicitis. Dr. Ken Gieser, who had interned in Dr. Bell's hospital in China, went to the hospital with her. When they operated on Rosa they discovered her abdominal cavity was filled with tubercular nodules. She had to have several months of complete bed rest. The housemother where Ruth and Rosa lived turned over the sunporch to the young patient and Ruth dropped out of school to care for her. She seemed to improve until just before she was to resume normal life when she hemorrhaged from her lungs and they knew she had tuberculosis all through her system. At the small hospital to which she was transferred, the surgeons proposed doing a phrenichotomy on one lung, permanently crushing the phrenic nerve, and a weekly pneumothorax treatment to rest the other.

At that time the Bells returned from China and moved Rosa to a drier climate at a hospital in New Mexico. Ruth stayed with Rosa and watched her attitude with interest. As Ruth said in later years, "There are two kinds of hypocrites in the world, one who wants you to think that they are better than they are and one who wants you to think they are worse than they are. Rosa was one of the latter. She delighted in shocking people. She read her Bible like some people read *Playboy* magazine, shoving it under her pillow when someone came into the room. However, she began to read her Bible in earnest and learned that while Jesus was here on earth, no one came to Him for healing without Jesus healing them. She read where James says, 'Is any one of you sick? He should call the elders of the church to pray over him and anoint him with oil in the name of the Lord. And the prayer offered in faith will make the sick person well' (James 5:14, 15). Rosa inquired and found a little church that followed those instructions; she called for the elders and they came and prayed for her. Rosa decided she could get up and lead a normal life and stopped the hospital treatments. Medically speaking, she should have hemorrhaged to death."

Ruth remembers her father's reaction to Rosa's decision: "Daddy was concerned. Being a doctor, he knew the dangers involved, but being a man of God he didn't want to discourage Rosa if God was leading her. He talked to the godly superintendent, Mrs. Van Devanter, who ran the hospital, and she said, 'Dr. Bell, there is something special happening in Rosa's life. I would be careful not to discourage it.'

"Rosa resumed a normal life, her lungs expanded, and to all appearances, she was healed. Later, the two doctors who had been treating her in New Mexico, both agnostics, said to Daddy, 'Dr. Bell, your daughter's explanation that God healed her is the only adequate one.'"

Ruth has said that, to her knowledge, from that day until this Rosa has never had a serious illness.

God does heal today and He often spares lives of some who, by human standards, would be dead. Our son, Franklin, has survived many harrowing circumstances, but one is especially vivid to us. This happened while he was a student at Le Tourneau College in Texas. He was taking flight instruction and during a spring break his flight instructor and wife, another buddy, and he flew down to Florida to join us for a few days' vacation. When they took off to return it was overcast. As they flew above the clouds, something happened to the electrical system and they lost all the lights on the plane. They descended beneath the cloud cover where they could see the lights of Jackson, Mississippi, and circled until they spotted a small airport. All the lights went on, the strobe lights were flashing, and they made a safe landing.

When the pilot walked over to thank the men in the tower for being so cooperative, they said, "We didn't even know you were coming . . . . We were just showing some friends around the airport and they wanted to know what would happen if someone came in late at night. We told them we'd turn on the strobe lights, so we demonstrated them. At that moment you came in sight and we couldn't believe it, because we didn't know there was a plane in the area."

God knew Franklin was not ready to go at that time. About two years later his flight instructor was killed in a crash. Sometimes God delivers us from death, and sometimes He doesn't. Only God knows the reason.

Ruth has a friend in England, Jennifer Larcombe, who had developed multiple sclerosis. She prayed for healing, but continued to get worse. She was besieged by people who told her that if everything was right between her and the Lord she would be healed, otherwise she must have some secret sin which she hadn't confessed. This advice was devastating to her, because she loved the Lord with all her heart. Finally, the British publishers, Hodder & Stoughton, asked her to write a book about her experiences. The book was eventually published and was called *Beyond Healing*. Ruth was asked to write the foreword, and when she read the manuscript she was deeply moved. Clearly, when God said no to Jennifer, He gave her another ministry.

James said, "And the prayer offered in faith will make the sick person well" (James 5:15). And, yet, James himself was beheaded. He trusted God, whatever the outcome.

Soon after James was put to death, Peter was arrested and put in prison. The believers prayed earnestly for Peter, and the night before he was to be brought to trial, an angel rescued him (Acts 12:5–11). In that situation, God said "yes" to Peter.

Christians know that God answers prayer in three ways: yes, no, and later. The apostles of Jesus illustrate this beautifully. After Pentecost, the early church was persecuted severely, but they trusted God in all circumstances. All but one of these apostles died as martyrs, but they were as faithful in their deaths as in their lives, understanding that death is the believer's translation to the presence of the Almighty.

Divine healing or deliverance from death is in His hands.

Sam was a devoted Christian who discovered that he had cancer of the mouth. As the dreadful disease developed, multiple operations took so much of his tongue and face that soon he had very little face left. His wife took him to a healing service and when they returned she told everyone triumphantly that Sam had been healed. It would be impossible to imagine what went on in Sam's mind as his suffering became worse. He hated to have anyone see him, and yet his wife would invite friends and neighbors in and announce that Sam was healed. Instead, he died. In such a case, an unrealistic faith in divine healing can be another form of denial: a belief that comes from disbelief in our own mortality.

Christians should have another view of divine healing, and that is to acknowledge God's ability to heal—but to be willing to accept a yes or no answer. Job was God's great example of this belief when he said, "Though he slay me, yet will I hope in him" (Job 13:15).

To face the awfulness of disease or illness, knowing that unless God intervenes we will die, is simply being honest.

The psalmist says, "The Lord will sustain him on his sickbed and restore him from his bed of illness" (Psalm 41:3). What a wonderful promise to know that God is with us, caring for us in the room where we are in pain. I have visited Christians in sickrooms where the presence of Christ was so real that, even in the midst of unbelievable suffering and facing death, the patient had serenity.

The Remarkable Amy Carmichael

In 1956 I was in India and visited the Tinnevelly district of South India where Amy Carmichael had lived. Amy was the first missionary to be supported by the Keswick Convention and a woman who wrote forty books during her lifetime. She labored in the land of her adoption for over fifty-six years, never once returning to her home in England on furlough.

I had the honor of visiting the place where she spent the last twenty years of her life, bedridden due to a leg injury from an accident. It was a modest little room, with red tile floor, very few pieces of furniture, and an enormous bird cage outside the window where she could watch the birds.

She had ministered and written from her bed for all those years, and I had a feeling of awe being shown the premises by the woman who had cared for her. As I stood in that simple place, the presence of Christ was very real. Amy went through the valley of the shadow and in spite of pain and physical weakness caused a great light to be spread around the world. It was during those years she did most of her writing—books that still bring blessing to millions across the world. Elisabeth Elliot has recently written her story in a challenging book entitled *A Chance to Die*

All Prayers Answered

Christians in desperate situations search the Scriptures for the many wonderful promises of God. One of our favorites is the statement made by Jesus that "You may ask me for anything in my name, and I will do it" (John 14:14). We claim that promise and ask the Lord to heal our loved one. But what happens if healing doesn't come? It's easy for Christians to feel guilty or believe our faith is weak if we pray for healing and it doesn't take place. Believers throughout the ages have had to face the fact that God does not heal everyone who prays for healing. But our lack of faith does not determine God's decision on healing. If that were so, He would have to apologize to all of His great servants in the Hebrews 11 Hall of Fame. Look at that cast of characters: Abel, Enoch, Noah, Abraham, Sarah, Isaac, Jacob, Joseph, Moses, Rahab, Gideon, Barak, Samson, Jephtah, David, Samuel, and all the prophets! All of these received great deliverance from God and endured incredible hardships through faith. What happened to them? "Some faced jeers and flogging, while still others were chained and put in prison. They were stoned; they were sawed in two; they were put to death by the sword. They went about in sheepskins and goatskins, destitute, persecuted and mistreated" (Hebrews 11:36, 37).

Even though God was pleased because of their faith,

they didn't receive much of the world's pleasures. Why? Because God had a better destination, a heavenly city, waiting for them. It was not because of lack of faith or as a punishment for sin that these men and women of God were not delivered from suffering and death. We have the faith to believe that God has a special glory for those who suffer and die for the sake of Christ.

The Pulpit on Death Row

Velma Barfield was a woman from rural North Carolina who was charged with first degree murder; no one could have surmised the effect her life and death would have upon so many people. In 1978 she was arrested for murdering four people, including her mother and fiancé. She never denied her guilt, but told the chilling story of her drug-dazed life, beginning with the tranquilizers which were prescribed following a painful injury.

Velma was a victim of incest as a child and the abuse of prescription drugs as an adult. After she admitted her guilt, she was taken to prison and confined in a cell by herself. One night the guard tuned in to a twenty-four-hour gospel station. Down the gray hall, desperate and alone in her cell, Velma heard the words of an evangelist and allowed Jesus Christ to enter her life. She wrote, "I had been in and out of churches all my life and I could explain all about God. But I had never understood before that Jesus had died for me."

Her conversion was genuine. For six years on death row she ministered to many of her cell-mates. The outside world began to hear about Velma Barfield as the story of her remarkable rehabilitation became known.

Velma wrote to Ruth and there developed a real friendship between them. In one letter Ruth wrote to Velma, "God has turned your cell on Death Row into a most unusual pulpit. There are people who will listen to what you have to say because of where you are. As long as God has a ministry for you here, He will keep you here. When I compare the dreariness, isolation, and difficulty of your cell to the glory that lies ahead of you, I could wish for your sake that God would say, 'Come on Home.'"[6]

My daughter, Anne, received special permission to visit Velma Barfield many times and was touched by the sadness of her story and the sincerity of her love for Christ as well as the beauty of her Christian witness in that prison.

Before her final sentence, Velma wrote to Ruth: "If I am executed on August 31, I know the Lord will give me dying grace, just as He gave me saving grace, and has given me living grace." On the night she was executed, Ruth and I knelt and prayed together for her till we knew she was safe in Glory.

Velma Barfield was the first woman in twenty-two years to be executed in the United States. She walked through the valley of the shadow for many years and at her memorial service the Reverend Hugh Hoyle said, "She died with dignity and she died with purpose. Velma is a living demonstration of 'by the grace of God you shall be saved.'"

Ruth wrote the following poem which was read for the benediction at Velma's funeral service:

> As the eager parents wait
> the homing of their child
> from far lands desolate,

from living wild;
wounded and wounding along the way,
their sorrow for sin ignored,
from stain and strain of night and day
to home assured.
So the Heavenly Father waits
the homing of His child;
thrown wide those Heavenly Gates
in welcome glorious-wild,
His, His the joy by right
—once crucified, reviled—
So precious in God's sight
is the death of His child.

Who Cares?

As Christians we are responsible for one another. "Carry each other's burdens, and in this way you will fulfill the law of Christ . . . . Therefore, as we have opportunity, let us do good to all people, especially to those who belong to the family of believers" (Galatians 6:2, 10). At no time is this more true than when suffering and death touch someone around us.

Often the friends and family who care for a sick loved one touch more lives by their example than they will ever know. But many times we are at a loss to know what to do, or what to say. We stumble in awkward embarrassment, or ignore an unpleasant situation by staying away from someone who is seriously ill. However, members of a family are not meant to suffer alone.

Most of us will have times in our lives when we are with people who are going through the valley of the shadow. How can we show the love of Christ? How would we like others to treat us if we were in similar

circumstances? Remember the words of Jesus: "In everything, do to others what you would have them do to you,
for this sums up the Law and the Prophets" (Matthew
7:12).

Margaret Vermeer served as a missionary in Nige-
ria. When she was seven months pregnant, she received
the report that a biopsy of a small tumor was malignant.
Five weeks after the surgery to remove the tumors, she
gave birth to a son, then began chemotherapy and radiation treatments. For two years she had a miraculous re-
mission, but then gradually more tumors appeared. As
her condition grew increasingly serious, she became
more sensitive about the way people viewed her. Six
months before she died she was speaking for women's
church groups, sharing her insights on how to care for
others as she wanted to be cared for. Here are some of
her thoughts:

First, be honest in sharing your feelings. Don't bounce
into the room with false cheerfulness, but admit your
helplessness and concern. "I would like to help you,
but I don't know how," is a straightforward expression of concern. Don't play games and be evasive.
Even children can cope better when people talk to
them honestly.

Don't preach a well-thought-out sermon. Christians
who bring out their Bibles and read lengthy passages are
not being sensitive. To share a verse that means something to you may be helpful, but wait for the signals
before plunging into a lengthy spiritual discussion.

Be a good listener. People will tell you what they are
ready to talk about. Sickness can be a very lonely journey.
When Jesus was agonizing in the Garden of Gethsemane,

He didn't want to face death alone. He asked three disciples to wait and pray with Him, but they fell asleep. What good were they?

Treat a dying person as a human being. Sometimes we treat a dying person in such a way that we make it harder on that person emotionally. We shut the people up in hospitals, whisper behind their backs, and deprive them of all the things that had made their lives rich. Familiar things *are* important.

One woman told me that when her mother was in a coma, she put a picture of her father, who had died many years before, on the nightstand beside her mother's bed. Whenever the comatose woman was turned to the other side, she struggled unconsciously to face the photograph of her husband. Finally, her daughter gave instructions to the nurse that whenever her mother was turned she was to move the picture, too. The woman never regained consciousness, but she died with a smile on her face, looking at the picture.

Provide spiritual support. When you quote a Bible verse to comfort a person, be sure you know what the verse means. When Margaret Vermeer knew that she only had a short time to live, she said that she was told by her Christian friends to "give thanks in all circumstances, for this is God's will for you in Christ Jesus" (1 Thessalonians 5:18). Does that mean to thank God for cancer? Didn't Jesus see sickness and disease as part of Satan's work? Look at the verse carefully. It doesn't say give thanks *for* everything, it says to give thanks *in* everything. There is a vast difference.

When we are told that "God causes everything to work together for good," it doesn't mean that all things are good in themselves, but that God is making them work out for good.

Always have hope. God is greater than the situations we face. Sometimes it's hard to find that which is positive and hopeful, but there is always something to be thankful for. Help the patient look forward to something . . . a visit from someone special . . . a time when you will be returning.

My mother loved to anticipate celebrations. A few months before she died, one of her granddaughters was going to be married. Her nurse knew that Mother was too weak to go to the wedding, but she helped her get dressed, anyhow, giving her the hope of that occasion. When Mother realized she couldn't go, she was at peace about it. If she had been told from the beginning that she couldn't make it, she would probably have been resentful.

Elisabeth Kübler-Ross made a great contribution to the understanding of death and dying, but her conclusions stand in stark contrast to the hope of the Christian. In an interview she was asked if a patient's religious orientation affected his view toward resignation in the end. She answered, "I have very few really religious people. The few I have—and I mean those with a deep intrinsic faith—have it much easier, but they are extremely few. Many patients become more religious in the end, but it is not really effective."[7]

My father-in-law, who had seen many die, said there was a vast difference between the reactions of believers and nonbelievers at the time of death.

In contrast to the anguish and anxiety of the person with no eternal hope, Christians can look to Christ for hope and encouragement. Because of our faith in Christ we do not ". . . grieve like the rest of men, who have no hope" (1 Thessalonians 4:13b).

Whatever suffering and agony we must endure, either in our own body or for someone we love, we are assured of His presence. And ultimately we will be resurrected with a body free of pain, an incorruptible and immortal body like His. This is our future hope.

The journey through the valley may be extremely difficult, but what a glorious destination awaits us when we travel with Jesus Christ!

6

HOW LONG IS

BORROWED TIME?

"There has always been a 'time to live and a time to die.'
Today, with the ability to prolong life, each one of us will
probably have to face this issue ourselves or with someone we
love. . . . . How long is too long?"

For the soul of every living thing is in the hand of God, and the breath of all mankind.

Job 12:10 LB

If I ever become so ill that only machines can keep me alive, please instruct the doctors to pull the plug."

Jacqueline Cole was forty-four years old when her husband, Presbyterian Minister Harry Cole, had to honor or ignore that agonizing request. Jacqueline had suffered a cerebral hemorrhage in the spring of 1986 and had been in a coma for forty-one days. When her case seemed hopeless, her husband reluctantly asked a Maryland judge to order doctors to let his comatose wife die, according to her own wishes. The judge determined that it was too soon to give up hope and six days later Jacqueline opened her eyes, smiled, and returned her husband's joyous kiss. "Miracles can and do occur," said the happy minister. "I guess we've muddied the waters surrounding the question of a person's right to die."[1]

Never before in human history has there been the urgency to debate such a vital and complex issue. There has always been a "time to be born and a time to die" (Ecclesiastes 3:2). Today, however, with the ability to prolong life, each one of us will probably have to face this issue ourselves or with someone we love. How long should we live on "borrowed time"? How long is too long? What are the medical, legal, and moral principles involved? What are the guidelines?

The issues of euthanasia and "right to die" will soon join the abortion issue as among the most vital and complicated concerns of our age.

We Have the Right to Die

Somehow we have confused the right to die with the subject of euthanasia (the deliberate killing of those who are suffering). They are not the same thing. The "right to die" is defined as the individual's right to determine whether unusual or "heroic" measures should be taken—normally involving expensive and mechanical means of life support—to prolong life in cases where death is almost certainly inevitable. Life is sacred and given to us by God; for that reason we must never condone the deliberate, unnatural taking of life. This is a major reason most Christians who take the Bible seriously oppose abortion and euthanasia. At the same time, allowing the natural process of death to run its course is not necessarily wrong, when life can only be sustained by extreme medical measures. There is a difference between the prolongation of life and the postponement of death.

Standing at the bedside of someone who has life-sustaining tubes intruding into many parts of the anatomy, we can understand how humane medical treatment could be viewed as inhumane. When the treatment of humans becomes, for all appearances, inhuman, most of us want the right to refuse such treatment.

Could you make a decision for yourself on whether or not life-sustaining procedures should be used? Members of the medical profession, the Los Angeles Bar Association, and the California Hospital Association gave some recommendations on withholding and withdrawing life-sustaining treatment. The first principle applies to each one of us. They said:

> It is the right of a person capable of giving informed consent to make his or her own decision regarding medical care after having been fully informed about the benefits, risks and consequences of available treatment, even if such a decision may result in shortening the individual's life.[2]

If we are able, we have the right to say, "Stop, no more."

A statement issued by American Catholic bishops in June 1986 said, "We also recognize and defend a patient's right to refuse 'extraordinary' means—that is, means which provide no benefit or which involve too grave a burden."[3]

But the right of choice by an individual is clouded. For instance, many people advocate drawing up a "living will" in anticipation of a time when they can no longer make decisions about sustaining or prolonging their lives. What is a living will? Is it something we should seriously consider in anticipation of a time when we cannot make a life or death decision for ourselves?

125

A living will is a document written and signed by a person at a time when he or she has the mental capacity to dictate final requests. Usually the living will states that "heroic measures" or artificial means should not be used if it has been determined that the person would remain in a vegetative state or in an irreversible coma.

On the surface this sounds like a good idea. Before such difficult decisions need to be made, why not clarify in advance how we wish to be treated? Unfortunately, it's not so simple. Right now I'm in reasonably good health. If I were to write a living will it would be from the perspective of how I think I would feel under more drastic circumstances. But when that time actually arrives, I might feel quite differently. Also, the guidelines set forth by the Joint Ad-Hoc Committee on Biomedical Ethics in California wisely say that "even when a competent patient has directed withholding or withdrawing of life-sustaining procedures, it is advisable to consult with the patient's immediate family and to give great weight to their wishes."

Finally, there is the question of whether "living wills" might not justify more questionable practices, such as euthanasia and suicide. The Bishops' Committee for Pro-Life Activities referred to such a possibility when they made their chilling statement: "Some living will proposals have been formulated and promoted by right-to-die groups which see them as stepping-stones to the eventual legalization of euthanasia."[4]

Our states do not agree upon the validity of "living wills." Proposals have been made, therefore, for uniform laws to eliminate the differences. But is federal legislation the answer? I cannot propose or evaluate such legislation, except to comment on ethical concerns. Would such legislation be in the interests of preserving life, preventing suicide and homicide, and maintaining sound ethics in the medical profession? That's a tall order! Would legislation encourage communication among patient, family, and physician in the decision-making process? Most important, are all of the considerations strongly biased toward life? All of these questions would need to be answered with a resounding "yes" before considering any so-called "right-to-die" legislation.

Each one of us needs to consider these subjects carefully and prayerfully and be alert to such issues as they become public matters. Also, we must each consider whether a "living will" is a document that we, ourselves, would want to write. And since these decisions affect our loved ones and families, it is important to discuss our feelings with them. And finally we must understand that, as it was for Jacqueline Cole, the final determination is in God's hand.

What Is "Passive Euthanasia"?

The phone rang and all conversation stopped. A friend of our family, who was at a bon voyage party for her upcoming departure for Europe for a writing assignment, had just finished telling of her concern for her mother who was on life-support systems in a distant state. Our friend had been assured by the doctors and members of her family that there was nothing she could do and that she should go on her trip as she had planned. Now the doctor was calling her long distance. "Your mother is in extreme discomfort, and it is the opinion of myself and the staff at the hospital that her condition is irreversible." He continued to describe her mother's condition and then asked the dreaded question, "Do you wish to have heroic efforts continued?"

"I don't know. I'll have to consult my brother," choked the distraught daughter. "Please tell me what 'heroic measures' means."

The doctor described the purpose and result of each tube, injection, and treatment. As the medical terminology was quoted, my friend began to shake and grow cold. "You're asking me to make a decision about killing my own mother," she cried.

Later, however, with the consent of her brother, the counsel of her minister, and a circle of prayer with her friends, the daughter told the doctor to discontinue the life-sustaining or "heroic" measures.

What my friend was forced to decide was when to permit what is termed today as "passive euthanasia." Although those words send shudders through most of us, the definition is important to understand. Passive or negative euthanasia means to discontinue or desist from the use of "extraordinary" life-sustaining measures or "heroic" efforts to prolong life in cases judged hopeless. It is refraining from action that would probably delay death and, instead, permitting death to occur naturally.

My friend's mother was then eighty-seven years old. To everyone's surprise, without the life-support systems she lived to be ninety-three. Even when we think we "play God," we may be fooled. The wisdom of God is greater than the foolishness of man.

Even the definitions of life-sustaining measures vary. A committee on biomedical ethics comprised of members of the medical and legal professions said: "Life-sustaining procedures are defined as interventions which artificially sustain, restore, or supplant a vital function and which serve only to artificially prolong the moment of death where, in the judgment of the attending physician, death is imminent whether or not such procedures are utilized."

In March of 1986 the American Medical Association Judicial Counsel gave the following opinion of "Withholding or Withdrawing Life-Prolonging Medical Treatment." Since most of us as laymen would not have access to this information, I think it is important to include it. This information was printed in the *Christian Medical Society Journal,* summer 1986.

The social commitment of the physician is to sustain life and relieve suffering. Where the performance of one duty conflicts with the other, the choice of the patient, or his family or legal representative if the patient is incompetent to act in his own behalf, should prevail. In the absence of the patient's choice or an authorized proxy, the physician must act in the best interest of the patient.

For humane reasons, with informed consent, a physician may do what is medically necessary to alleviate severe pain, or cease or omit treatment to permit a terminally ill patient whose death is imminent to die. However, he should not intentionally cause death. In deciding whether the administration of potentially life-prolonging medical treatment is in the best interest of the patient who is incompetent to act in his own behalf, the physician should determine what the possibility is for extending life under humane and comfortable conditions and what are the prior expressed wishes of the patient and attitudes of the family or those who have responsibility for the custody of the patient.

Even if death is not imminent but a patient's coma is beyond doubt irreversible and there are adequate safeguards to confirm the accuracy of the diagnosis and with the concurrence of those who have responsibility for the care of the patient, it is not unethical to discontinue all means of life-prolonging medical treatment.

Life-prolonging medical treatment includes medication and artificially or technologically supplied respiration, nutrition or hydration. In treating a terminally ill or irreversibly comatose patient, the physician should determine whether the benefits of treatment outweigh its burdens. At all times, the dignity of the patient should be maintained.[5]

These legal guidelines are, according to a Christian doctor, "very permissive toward withdrawal of all life-sustaining measures."

Most of the time I see issues as right or wrong, black or white. However, searching for God's will in the matter of life-sustaining measures is perhaps one of the most difficult decisions we will ever have to make. The prestigious *New England Journal of Medicine* said "few topics in medicine are more complicated, more controversial, and more emotionally charged than treatment of the hopelessly ill. Technology competes with compassion, legal precedent lags, and controversy is inevitable" ("The Physician's Responsibility toward Hopelessly Ill Patients," 310:955–959).

The doctors' dilemma is our dilemma, too. It is a complicated, emotionally charged issue which many of us may encounter in our lifetimes.

What Is "Active Euthanasia"?

Active euthanasia is an act of commission, rather than omission. Its proponents contend it is a positive merciful act taken deliberately to end futile suffering or a meaningless existence; it could involve lethal drugs or the withholding of nourishment. Christians, however, would strongly disagree with this view.

In most cases, this constitutes a criminal act. But not always. Take the case of author Betty Rollin, who revealed her role in helping her mother commit suicide.

In the spring of 1986, the New York writer told a luncheon meeting of women how she provided the capsules which ended her mother's life. The elder woman had ovarian cancer and had pleaded with her daughter to help her die. "Rollin and her husband called dozens of doctors across the country before an Amsterdam physician gave them a combination of pills that would be lethal, yet painless."[6]

In her book about this experience, Betty Rollin wrote about how she came to make such a decision and how she dealt with the implications of it. Later, it was reported, "Rollin calmly said, 'I knew that at worst I would be arrested. And that at best I wouldn't be arrested.'" As far as I know, she was never arrested, nor did she face much opposition in her act.

Where do we go from here? Are we just a breath away from euthanasia on demand? There are groups in America and many other nations who vocally support it as a means of preserving "human dignity" and eliminating needless suffering.

Some doctors have also gone on record in support of active euthanasia. Dr. Christiaan Barnard gained a great deal of notoriety after performing the first heart transplant. His views on euthanasia and suicide were published a few years ago in a book, *Good Life, Good Death*. He writes, "I have no deep conviction in the existence of a personal God or in the geography of an actual heaven or hell. To that I must add, on the other hand, that I have not dismissed the possibility of life after death."[7]

Dr. Barnard said that he never practiced active euthanasia, since in his country it is regarded as murder and could merit the death penalty. But, on the other hand, he says, "I believe that in the clinical practice of medicine, active euthanasia has a definite place."[8]

Ten thousand irreversibly comatose patients are currently institutionalized in America, according to medical estimates. When the AMA stated its guidelines on the discontinuance of life-prolonging treatment, one of the statements included withdrawal of medication and artificially or technologically supplied respiration, nutrition, or hydration. Now we are talking about food and water.

Elizabeth Bouvia, a quadriplegic cerebral palsy patient, made national headlines in her fight to be allowed to starve to death. At first a judge refused her request. She became the object of bitter legal battling. While hospital officials and the American Civil Liberties Union took sides, the public debate brought the issue into the open. Finally a California appeals court ordered the removal of her feeding tube. As of this writing, however, she is still alive by her own choice.

But there is more at stake here than the life of one individual. Some have said that removal of food and fluids is frighteningly reminiscent of Nazi Germany where "useless mouths" weren't fed. Dr. Leo Alexander, consultant to the office of the Chief of Counsel for War Crimes wrote about how German physicians started a trend which resulted in the euthanasia of 275,000 people before the war began:

It started with the acceptance of the attitude, basic in the euthanasia movement, that there is such a thing as a life not worthy to be lived. This attitude in its early stages concerned itself merely with the severely and chronically sick. Gradually the sphere of those to be included in this category was enlarged to encompass the socially unproductive, the ideologically unwanted, the racially unwanted, and finally all non-Germans. But it is important to realize that the infinitely small wedged-in lever from which this entire trend of mind received its impetus was the attitude toward the nonrehabilitatable sick.[9]

I am not so sure it couldn't happen again. Even the possibility is enough to keep us ever vigilant against attempts to encourage or promote euthanasia.

The Inevitable Will of God

There is a rising tide of opinion in favor of active euthanasia. Prominent physicians are heard to say that "prolonging life is cruel." As compassionate as this observation may seem on the surface, there are important biblical standards which both Christians and non-Christians must consider.

From the biblical perspective, we know that death is inevitable, but not to be hastened. Human life is given by God and is precious. "I praise you because I am fearfully and wonderfully made; your works are wonderful, I know that full well" (Psalm 139:14). God can and may intervene to restore someone who was considered a terminal patient. "I put to death and I bring to life, I have wounded and I will heal, and no one can deliver from my hand" (Deuteronomy 32:39).

133

"Lord, let me die," is a prayer and a plea offered to God by many throughout the ages. Moses was not ill, but he was grieved about the burden the Lord had given him. He looked at his people grumbling about their food and their living conditions, complaining until Moses must have reached his limit. He'd had it. He said to God, "If this is how you are going to treat me, put me to death right now" (Numbers 11:15).

But the Lord was not finished with Moses yet! He went on to lead his people through the wilderness and to the boundaries of the Promised Land.

Elijah had killed the prophets of Baal, yet when the evil Queen Jezebel swore she was going to get even, the fearless Elijah ran into the wilderness, sat down under a juniper tree, and cried out, "I have had enough, Lord," he said. "Take my life; I am no better than my ancestors" (1 Kings 19:4).

But the Lord sent an angel to supply him with food and water; essential ingredients for life!

The Lord was not finished with Elijah yet.

And think about Job. He had boils all over his body. His flesh was eaten by worms. His skin was oozing and decaying like rotten turnips. He was so shriveled and thin that his bones were sticking out and he had gnawing pains and frightening dreams. Under such circumstances, most of us would cry out, as Job did, "that God would be willing to crush me, to let loose his hand and cut me off!" (Job 6:9).

But the Lord was not finished with Job yet, either.

If we had been with Job in his pain-wracked, miserable situation, would we have taken away his food and water, and allowed him to starve and dehydrate?

The Bible does not give us clear-cut answers on

134

how to treat people in a "vegetative" state. However, the Scriptures are very clear about caring for the weak and defenseless. While "pulling the plug" may not result in death, denying food and water means certain death.

Dr. David Schiedermayer, from the Center for Clinical Ethics, Pritzer School of Medicine, University of Chicago, said, "Our courts and our society are rapidly moving toward approving the withdrawal of food and water from patients. As a clinician and as a Christian, I share the concerns of many who feel this is morally wrong. If this is not the time to speak up, then there will never be a time. Food and water have always been worth fighting about."[10]

While all must sympathize with human suffering, practicing "active euthanasia," either through the use of lethal drugs or denial of food and water, violates the Judeo-Christian code of moral conduct.

Is Suicide the Way to Go?

The old Eskimo is sick and knows he is dying. He walks out into the cold, killing world and falls into a freezing slumber. His family did not abandon him. They supported him in this act of suicide. It was their way of life—and death.

To many peoples of the earth, death is intimately related to group survival. Legends from Iceland, Greenland, and Siberia tell us that suicide is normal when life has no other meaning.

Ritual suicide was practiced by peoples of Africa and South America where the deaths of wives, servants, and members of the court would follow the death of the king. Of the major world religions, Shintoism,

Buddhism, and Hinduism allow suicide, but Catholicism and Judaism condemn it.

Today, suicide is committed in startling numbers by teen-agers, cutting short promising young lives. Men and women take their own lives to avoid the problems or responsibilities of living. In many cases serious emotional illness is involved, in which the person may not be fully rational or responsible for his or her actions. Others, a smaller percentage, are the people who are severely ill and near death, who seek a way of escape.

Suicide is a crime in America, as is attempted suicide. Aiding a suicide is tantamount to homicide. But there are those who lobby to make it a legal and acceptable possibility.

A few years ago *Time* magazine had a story about a British society which issued a pamphlet on "How to Commit Suicide." It listed methods, gave specific drugs, and advised against such methods as shooting, slashing wrists, or jumping from buildings.

This is a painful issue for many people who struggle with feelings of despair and hopelessness. And while the Bible does not give us detailed direction on this subject, it does come down firmly on the side of life and hope, and that should inform us as we consider this and the many related issues.

In many cases, the real burden of suicide falls upon those who are left behind. Anne-Grace Scheinin, a woman who had attempted suicide many times, wrote a strong argument against taking one's own life. She spoke from personal experience, using the example of her own mother who had committed suicide: "There is something about suicide that, even when done as an escape from an agonizing terminal illness, signals complete and utter defeat. It is without any semblance of nobility or pride. Life can become too heavy a burden to bear, but the release that suicide offers is not a triumph of life, the ultimate mastery of self over fate, but a grim renunciation of hope and a failure of the human spirit."

This California woman wrote, "No matter how bad the pain is, it's never so bad that suicide is the only answer . . . suicide doesn't end pain. It only lays it on the broken shoulders of the survivors." And she ends her story. "By the way: to all the doctors, nurses and psychiatrists who forced me to live when I didn't want to—thank you for keeping breath in my lungs and my heart beating and encouraging hope in me when I didn't have any hope."[11]

If we are made in God's image, do we have the human right to destroy our own bodies? Every day we commit little acts of suicide in the manner in which we care for those bodies, but these are not the overt acts of taking our own lives.

A Broadway and London hit play, "Whose Life Is It Anyway?" treated suicide and mercy killing in a sympathetic manner.[12]

This issue is a struggle against "the powers of this dark world and against the spiritual forces of evil" described in Ephesians 6:12. Little by little, the sanctity of life is being eroded. Will survival of the fittest be our elitist philosophy? I pray not!

Questions to Ask

In his poignant book, which he called *Mother's Song*, John Sherrill relates the decision he had to make concerning the life and death of his mother. When her death seemed imminent and he could not bear to see her suffer, he asked the doctor, "What would happen if we asked for those IVs to come out?"

Sherrill said he tensed for what he expected as an outraged reaction from the doctor. Instead, the doctor gave him some yardsticks to consider. With the prayerful agreement of the entire family and the concurrence of the doctor, he eventually asked to have his mother's life-prolonging measures removed. He summed up some important questions to ask ourselves now, while we are healthy and alert. This is what he listed:

1. If doctors are able to help an elderly person through a health crisis, what does he return to? Will it be to a life of reason and tolerable health, or will it be to new breakdown and deterioration and pain?
2. What does the person himself want? Has he expressed a desire to live just as long as possible, no matter what the means? Or does he want to be allowed to die without using the extraordinary aids that are available to us today?
3. What is the person's attitude now? Our feelings may change as death approaches. Even if we are unable to speak there are innumerable ways to communicate . . .
4. What is the attitude of the family?
5. What is God's timing? We found that His signature is beauty, even in the midst of pain and sorrow. In Mother's passing we encountered example after example (coincidences, kindnesses, unusual provisions). They were His encouragements, we believe now, that we had correctly interpreted the signs of His time.

Is death the end? This is the question, of course, that affects all the others. Facing death is entirely different for someone who believes that there is an afterlife.[13]

138

Yes, we need to know the right questions to ask, for we live on borrowed time, and we want to use our inheritance as wisely as we can. Since God has given us sound minds, we must exercise them while they are able to function. This is not morbid, this is one of the greatest challenges we may ever face.

> When death comes
> will it come quietly
> —one might say creep—
> as after a hard
> and tiring day, one lies
> and longs for sleep—
> ending age and sorrow
> or youth and pain?
> Who dies in Christ
> has all to gain
> —and a Tomorrow!
> Why weep?
> Death may be savage.
> We cannot be sure:
> the godly may be slaughtered,
> evil men endure;
> however death may strike,
> or whom,
> who knows the risen Lord
> knows, too, the empty tomb.

—Ruth Bell Graham[14]

7

LIFE AND DEATH

CHOICES

"Most of us have a subliminal desire to leave this world with some degree of dignity . . . quick, quiet, easy. But life doesn't follow the pattern we have so clumsily designed. . . . Death has many faces and voices."

If any of you lacks wisdom, he should ask God, who gives gener-
ously to all without finding fault, and it will be given to him.

James 1:5

Wisdom to make choices in life . . . and in approaching death. How we need God's wisdom. For instance,
most of us have a subliminal desire to leave this world
with some degree of dignity . . . perhaps at the age of
ninety-five, sitting in an easy chair before a fire . . . just
close our eyes and the next thing we know we're in eternity. Quick, quiet, and easy.

But life doesn't follow the pattern we have so clumsily designed. "Why, you do not even know what will
happen tomorrow. What is your life? You are a mist that
appears for a little while and then vanishes" (James 4:14).

Most of us would like to say something quotable to
be remembered by our family. But what if disease or age
ravages our body and the person in the mirror shows

little resemblance to the snapshot in the family album? Is it possible to say good-bye to earthly life with some degree of honor?

A doctor painted two verbal portraits of undignified death for me. The first he described in this way: "The ICU death: comatose, respirator keeping the shell of a body alive indefinitely, a few EEG waves flickering here and there keeping it going, two or three IVs, tubes in the nose and bladder, multiple consultants making daily adjustments to keep the numbers balanced, and the bill increasing by $2,000 a day with no end in sight."

A grim thought! And yet it happens with increasing frequency. Alan's case is one example. For months Alan was sustained in just that manner. His insurance was used up and his money all gone. At that point his wife prayed for his death and, finally, stopped coming to see him altogether. When Alan died he left her a legacy of bitterness and regret.

The cases are legion on hospital records. Death's sting may be cruel and lingering and financially devastating.

The second portrait of undignified death may be viewed on occasion in a nursing home. For weeks, months, or years the patient depends upon employees of an institution, who may or may not have much interest in her comfort. Her surroundings consist of a bed, bed table, the moans and babblings from the next room (or the next bed), the aroma of disinfectant trying to cover the unpleasant odors. When death finally comes, a distant relative is notified, who then puts on a sad voice and makes the arrangements over the phone.

Unfortunately, the description, and the fact, is too common. Ask any nursing home manager and he will tell you about Mrs. Thomas or Mr. Peters who has been in the home for years, with only token visits from anyone who cares. Many people are abandoned socially long before they die physically.

Nursing homes can be a great blessing to people who find it impossible to care for their elderly or infirm family members at home. However, careful investigation should be made to assure the family and patient that dignified treatment is the order of the day. One friend told me how his mother had died in a "rest home" and when he went to pick up her belongings he was directed to a storage room where he found a plastic trash bag stuffed with her pictures, plants, and clothing. His grief was compounded by those thoughtless actions.

This is not an indictment of nursing homes. Most are wonderful, run by caring, compassionate personnel. I visited Vance Havner, the noted Bible preacher, who was in a fine establishment in his last days.

However, in contrast to abandonment or undignified treatment, picture homy surroundings, with a few friends or close family members nearby, personal affairs settled, and a certainty of a future with a loving God.

After Ruth's father died, her mother found it increasingly difficult to take care of herself. She was partly paralyzed by a stroke, dependent upon help for most of her physical needs. Ruth had her brought up to our mountain home for a while, but she wanted her own home, so that's where she was returned.

Ruth said, "All her life Mother loved music—both playing the piano and singing, as well as listening to others make music."

Then during her final days, we suddenly realized that hymns enjoyed by the living do not necessarily appeal to the dying. Ruth went through her favorite record albums, marking hymns she felt her mother would enjoy, and our local radio station graciously lifted them off onto tapes. As Ruth recalled those days, she said, "Mother had a simple tape player and was able to push the on and off button at will, so beautiful old hymns ministered to her hour after hour the last few weeks she was with us."

Harder Decisions

We did not have to make the difficult decision with Ruth's mother whether to sustain or prolong her life. She was not on life-support systems, but she needed complete and loving care. There was no question in our minds but that was what she would have.

We have a close friend who had to make the decision for her husband whether his life would be sustained by machines or not. Fortunately, they had discussed the possibility of this choice before the time of crucial need.

Edith Schaeffer, the widow of my friend, the late Francis Schaeffer, was called into the hospital room of her husband who was dying of cancer. Six doctors told her there was little hope for Francis, and they asked her if she wanted him placed in intensive care on machines. One doctor, acting as spokesman, said, "Once a person is on machines, I would never pull the plug. I need to know what your viewpoint is."

Edith knew that for years she and Francis had talked about the preciousness of life and that even a few minutes could make a difference if something needed to be said or done. "But," she said, "there is no point in simply prolonging death. It is a fine line; it is not an absolute one-two-three process. There are differences from person to person, and it requires great wisdom."

Edith Schaeffer chose to have her husband brought home. She said, "I believe when my husband leaves his body, he will be with the Lord. I don't want him to leave me until he's with the Lord. Therefore, I am sure he would want to go to the house he asked me to buy and be there for the time he has left."

The doctors agreed with her and told her they wished more people would do things the same way. Fran was taken home, and Edith surrounded his bed with the things he loved, and had music playing in his room. She said, "One after another, we played his favorite records: Beethoven, Bach, Schubert, and Handel. Ten days later, on May 15, 1984, with the music of Handel's *Messiah* still in the air, Fran breathed his last breath."[1]

A Public Death

I remember a man who added a new dimension to the idea of dying with dignity. Hubert Humphrey was vice president of the United States under Lyndon Johnson. He established his career and reputation as a Senator, and later as the Democratic party's unsuccessful presidential candidate. However, Humphrey made some of his greatest public statements in his dying months when he became a role model for the American public.

Do you remember when cancer was too often a whispered word? Perhaps more than anyone else, Humphrey brought the dreaded subject out of the closet. In 1977 his doctors made public the diagnosis, and we understand it was with his approval. He had an inoperable tumor and his situation was terminal. One of the nation's leading writers and teachers on death and dying, Edwin Shneidman, wrote, "Thereafter, the world either had to shun Humphrey as a leper and pariah (because of the social stigma of terminal cancer) or, because of who he was and the way in which he conducted himself, accept him as he was."[2]

The public accepted Humphrey, and watched his attitude as he approached death openly and with wry humor. "The extraordinary public death from cancer of Hubert Humphrey can be a guiding example to some of one kind of 'appropriate death.' His published utterances about his cancer, his state of health, and his death probably can stimulate many of us to think about our own way of dying."[3]

Humphrey's remarks on the floor of the Senate express so beautifully the qualities that make for a dignified, graceful death. He said, "The greatest healing therapy is friendship and love, and over this land I have sensed it. Doctors, chemicals, radiation, pills, nurses, therapists are all very, very helpful. But without faith in yourself and your own ability to overcome your own difficulties, faith in divine providence, and without the friendship and kindness and generosity of friends, there is no healing."[4]

He knew he would not be healed, but he expressed what is needed by all of us . . . friendship, kindness, and faith in God.

Different People, Different Choices

We know that death has many faces and voices. Paul Tournier wrote, "Rare is the death that is truly conscious, lucid, serene, and accepted. But how impressive such a death is! A young woman with whom I have worked for a long time falls seriously ill in the flower of life. From the start she feels intuitively that she will not recover. She makes out a list of the relatives and friends whom she wants to see once more before she goes, and invites them one by one to her bedside. She prays that she will be able to give to each the message she has in her heart for them, and dies the day after the last visit. I have myself been called for in this way by several of my best friends, when they knew their days to be numbered. At such times how profound the dialogue between us becomes!"[5]

Most people die somewhere between the two extremes of death: the dignified and the utterly undignified. Increasing longevity, advances in public health, and improved sanitation, along with the likelihood of a reasonably safe environment for older citizens in recent decades mean that the most common causes of death among the elderly are degenerative illnesses such as cardiovascular disease, cancer, strokes, diabetic complications, and other disorders.

But we're seeing two trends in major medical care. One is a tendency for doctors to overtreat the patient with cautious but expensive care in order to protect themselves against the potential threat of malpractice suits. This can lead to "heroic medical treatment" in some cases. At the opposite extreme, there is the pragmatic approach which says if the person is not useful, withhold even minimal care. A Christian doctor said, "The latter is going to become more tempting as money becomes tighter and as individual human life becomes devalued."

So, what is the answer? Can we find a moderate and

loving position which guarantees the dignity of the patient during the period of disease and convalescence without destroying that dignity with expensive, exhaustive, and unproductive treatment?

Dr. C. Everett Koop, surgeon general of the United States, said, "All such talk has different connotations for the Christian than for the non-Christian. My wife knows I do not believe in being ushered out of this life with a lethal injection. I want to hang around long enough to be sure my family is taken care of. But after that, I don't want my life prolonged in great discomfort when it is fruitless."[6] Dr. Koop is also a great Bible student.

God's Wisdom and Our Responsibility

A sick person has God-given worth. God is concerned about the way we treat people who may not have much to offer us. An influential or public figure may have little trouble getting kind and loving treatment. But when Jesus was teaching His disciples He said, "For I was hungry and you gave me something to eat, I was thirsty and you gave me something to drink, I was a stranger and you invited me in, I needed clothes and you clothed me, I was sick and you looked after me, I was in prison and you came to visit me" (Matthew 25:35, 36).

His followers were baffled. When had they done all of those noble deeds? Jesus told them, "I tell you the truth, whatever you did for one of the least of these brothers of mine, you did for me" (Matthew 25:40).

Let's take a look at some of the ways we can contribute to the God-given worth of a human life . . . and how we would want to be treated ourselves.

Please Don't Leave Me

I have often said that loneliness is the predominant attitude in our culture. A person can be lonely in the midst of a party; he can be lonely in a crowd or lonely in the country. Loneliness may be experienced by the rich and famous or the poor and unknown. Loneliness may engulf the dying and make their last hours a torture chamber of abandonment. How can this be? It is because of certain attitudes others assume.

First, there is the monologue attitude. "How are you today, Bill? You look fine." Bill is ready to tell how he feels and needs to express some of his concerns, but the "stiff upper lip" syndrome has been imposed upon him by his doctor or his friends. They inform him how he ought to feel and then may say, "I'll be back to see you again." The promise is made, but not kept, in the same way some Christians say piously, "I'll pray for you," and then never do.

Another attitude promotes a sense of abandonment. A person may be treated as though disease or an accident has turned him into a nonperson. Just as we sometimes do to children, we talk in front of them as if they weren't even there. Even my dogs have the intelligence to know when we are talking about them. They will turn their heads to one side and their ears will prick up. Jesus was talking about "the least of these," and even animal lovers will agree that humans have higher intelligence than dogs.

People who are asking for help give cues. We need to be sensitive to them. "I think I'm going to die soon," is a plea for understanding, not a statement to disregard.

Too many times we respond with nonsense, such as, "You're going to live many years more," when all of the indications are to the contrary. Honesty seems to fly out of many sickroom windows.

Sometimes people in nursing homes, as well as terminally ill patients, are truly abandoned. "I'd rather remember her as she was," is the rationalization. Another indication of this abandonment has to do with physical contact. First, the loved one is kissed on the lips, then the kiss drops lightly on the forehead, the next time it is blown from across the room, and loneliness grows.

I wonder what would have happened if Jacob's family had abandoned him? In his last days he gathered all of his sons around him and prophesied what would happen to each one of them. Some of them received strong admonitions, others blessings. When he was finished, the Bible says that Jacob "breathed his last and was gathered to his people" (Genesis 49:33).

One Choice for the Terminally Ill

Several years ago Columnist George Will wrote a *Newsweek* article called "A Good Death." I cut the piece out and kept it because I wanted to know what he considered a *good* death and a *bad* one, and I found some of his commentary indicative of popular American attitudes on human dignity.

Will said, "There comes a point in a degenerative disease when further 'aggressive' treatment would intensify the patient's suffering without substantial benefit. Then concern for the patient should become concern for a dignified death."[7]

The article continued with a description of the

hospice program. This is a new-old concept that is growing rapidly in the Western world. It is comparatively new in America, but old in following the Christian principles of the Golden Rule.

During the Middle Ages, medieval hospices were refuges where pilgrims were sheltered and fed along their long journey to the Holy Land. Sometimes hospices were located near monasteries. One of the most famous was the hospice of St. Bernard in the Swiss Alps. (We think of the massive St. Bernard with the flask around his huge neck as being a dog that saved lives, and that was true at one time.)

The modern hospice movement began in England, where a caring woman, Dr. Cicely Saunders, founded St. Christopher's, the model upon which so many others have been based. A hospice provides care for terminally ill patients and their loved ones; its primary purpose is to alleviate chronic pain. One hospice medical director said, "There is never a time when nothing more can be done. There may be nothing more that can be done to cure the disease, but there are always further measures to be taken for the comfort of the patient."

The purpose of St. Christopher's is to render loving care, using medicine with a humane dimension in the treatment of all aspects of pain: physical, social, emotional, and spiritual. The hospice is a therapeutic community within the community, helping the dying to live until they die and helping families to live on.

George Will commented, "With hospice care as an alternative, there would be little demand for euthanasia. Without the hospice alternative, legalization of euthanasia would exert vicious pressure on people who are old and frail and believe society does not think much of them. When incurably ill, such people would think of an administered death as the only alternative to terrible suffering for themselves and terrible cost to their families, so their right to die would come to seem like a 'duty to die.'"[8]

What does a dying person want? The material things which were once so important become insignificant. Tournier said, "The pursuit of success, the hard struggle to avoid failure, is appropriate enough in the prime of life. But whatever fruit this long effort has borne, it will seem of small account in the face of approaching death. What counts then is serenity."[9]

Serenity is the "quiet waters" of the Twenty-third Psalm. Serenity is what the old man, Simeon, expressed when the child Jesus was presented to him: "Lord," he said, "now I can die content" (Luke 2:29 LB).

Serenity is what the devoted people in the hospice movement wish to bring to the dying. Serenity and dignity.

Special Care for Special People

The hospice movement continues to grow. If you know someone in a life-threatening or terminal illness, you may find that a hospice offers a reasonable and considerate alternative for care.

What qualifies someone for hospice care? When a physician determines there is nothing more that he can do to save a person's life, he may recommend a hospice instead of hospital care. Anyone can refer a patient to hospice care. In most cases, the dying person stays at home and a support team, consisting of doctors, nurses, medical social workers, chaplains, home health aides, and trained volunteers, provides individualized, comprehensive care. The teamwork does not cease with death, but continues to help the family during bereavement.

San Diego has a hospice program which was started by sixty people who were concerned for dying patients and their families. In less than ten years the concept continued to grow until more than 3,200 patients and families had been served. Today, if the criteria have been met—which simply means a person must be diagnosed as having a terminal illness, with only days, weeks, or, at the most, months left to live—anyone can get help. Color, creed, or financial status is neither a deterrent nor a qualification for admission to such a facility.

Deep human needs surface when someone is dying. Sometimes the family feels helpless, and at other times they are angry. Emotions may be hidden, only to surface in painful outbursts. "The hospice goal is to assist in the emergence of these positive and natural feelings so that one's last passage is as it should be—free from pain and stress, in an atmosphere of love and caring."[10]

The public relations director of the San Diego Hospice, and the chaplain, emphasized that the role of all the team and volunteers is to combine care with caring.

Among some of the home care services are daily home visits, assistance in personal and business affairs, nursing care, running errands, and spiritual and psychological support. After the death of the patient, the hospice continues offering help to the family during their grief.

One story was told about an attitude change brought about by a member of a hospice team. I heard about a grandfather who was dying. His four-year-old granddaughter was ordered to go to another part of the house to play, and told not to go near Grandpa's room. The adult members of the family sat and cried in the living room, and the teenage grandsons wandered in and out of the house aimlessly. A hospice worker found the little girl sobbing in the corner of her room. "What's the matter, honey?" she asked.

"They won't let me see Grandpa, and I'm scared," she whimpered. "I think they're going to do something awful to him."

The hospice nurse went to the family and said, "It's wrong not to allow the children to see their grandfather and tell him good-bye. Don't keep them away."

Reluctantly, the mother and father told their children they could go into the room. The little girl stood on her tiptoes and kissed her Grandpa, and then, not satisfied that he knew she was there, she pulled herself up on the bed and snuggled next to him. The boys sat in chairs beside his bed, and a smile came to Grandpa's face—and he died peacefully.

That little girl will never forget the experience, her love for her grandfather, or being there beside him the last few minutes of his life.

Experience in England shows that hospice care has other good effects. Depression, anxiety, and anger are reduced, with those who are cared for in homes. One of the things that has happened in areas where the hospice movement is working is that more people are now dying at home. In New Haven, Connecticut, for instance, the statistics changed from about ten percent dying at home to over seventy percent. A positive direction has been added to our society with the staffs and volunteers in this outstanding effort. I hope many more Christians will become involved in this movement, as a means of witnessing to Christ's love.

Opportunity to Show Christ's Love

Remember the story of Jesus and the blind man told in the ninth chapter of John? Here is a model of needs being met and eyes opened to a personal relationship with the Lord. The man was blind and Jesus healed him. The Pharisees were shocked that Jesus healed him on the sabbath, and they scorned him. But the once-blind man knew that the man who healed him had a special relationship with God, and he wanted to know more about this source of comfort and love.

When a person's needs are met, it may open his eyes or improve his vision to what God can accomplish in his life. God gives us the example through Jesus, and we are following Him when we get involved with something as positive as this recent trend on the American caring scene. It is Christ ministering to others through His own. If the current dire predictions come true concerning deaths from the AIDS virus, the need for more programs like this will become urgent.

Many times the dying child unwittingly directs his parents toward the Lord. The chaplain of one hospice said that he wished older persons could have the insight which dying children often have. "Children are so open to talking about God. They are more willing to talk about dying than their elders."

At some point, terminal patients have to come to grips with their condition. However, in the past the families and the patients were usually left to tough it out with little support, especially when they had no religious background or involvement. Now that this is changing, the Christian community should take note and do something. For instance, direct care volunteers are needed by all hospices. They are called "The Heart of the Hospice."

The direct care volunteer is a special friend to patients and their families.

Patient care volunteers are trained in such topics as communication, pain and symptom control, grief and bereavement support, spiritual care, ethical issues, and terminal care. Although these skills may sound complicated, they are essential human qualities, talents we all possess to some degree. They are an expression of the compassion which can help many thousands of people (as people live longer in this latter part of the twentieth century) to attain some degree of dignity in their last days.

Most important of all, we should be willing to pray with those in their final days and hours and read to them from the Scriptures. Remember that it is through "the encouragement of the Scriptures we might have hope" (Romans 15:4).

Jesus is walking the earth today in the hearts of those who believe in Him. More good has been done, more people loved, more comfort brought by His people than by the humanistic philosophy that displays a caring philosophy without His saving grace.

"Christians Who Care" should be the slogan, and the banner, for the body of believers. When others see the compassion we express for the suffering and bereaved, they will truly believe our faith means something. In the words of the song, "They will know we are Christians by our love, by our love; yes, they'll know we are Christians by our love."

8

GROPING

THROUGH GRIEF

"The façade of grief may be indifference, preoccupation, anger, cheerfulness, or any variety of emotions. But if we try to understand it, we may learn how to cope with it."

That their hearts might be comforted, being knit together in love. . . .

Her son was dead, killed in a tragic accident only a few days before. She sat in the front row of the church, listening quietly as the minister spoke at the memorial service, her face composed, one might almost say serene. When the final prayer ended, friends filed by the casket, hugging members of the family through tears. Later it was said, "They are taking it so well." "His mother is a real brick." At the home afterward, the parents greeted dozens of people with smiles and words of encouragement.

A few days later her husband found his wife sitting on the kitchen floor, banging her fists and sobbing uncontrollably. The woman others thought was "so brave" was sick to the core of her being with an emotion common to every living person.

A neighbor of ours, whom we'll call Frances North, lost her husband through a tragic accident. Again, everyone commented on the widow's bravery—even cheerfulness.

"Only the Lord can give such victory," was the general opinion. Perhaps poor Frances felt trapped. How could she express her grief without letting the Lord down?

Months passed, and Ruth got a phone call. A friend was concerned. Frances was withdrawing more and more into herself.

So Ruth, having been friends with Frances for years, drove over. She found Frances sitting alone, staring at the floor. Gently, Ruth talked with her and received either no response or one in monosyllables. Finally, realizing Frances was worse off than she had thought, Ruth asked if she would like her to call the doctor. Frances nodded numbly. Ruth called and was told to bring her right over.

The doctor, an understanding, compassionate Christian, recognized the danger signals of unresolved, long suppressed grief, and took her under his care.

Today Frances is the normal, happy, outgoing person she was before tragedy struck.

How wrong we may be when we draw conclusions about others based on their outward appearance or attitude. Peel away the smile and you may uncover a desperate need. Grief hides under many masquerades. It takes many forms. The façade of grief may be indifference, preoccupation, anger, cheerfulness, or any variety of emotions. But if we try to understand it, we may learn how to cope with it. When we experience it, we may be able to help others.

Grief Is a Fact

Grief comes with many losses. It may be the loss of a job or a friend, a pet or a possession. The loss of a marriage relationship may cause grief as wrenching as death. Whatever its cause, grief will come to all of us.

Statistics reveal that grief-causing sorrow affects ten families out of every 250 each year in America. Since we are studying the subject of death and dying, we will look particularly at personal grief, and how to comfort someone who is grieving, in relation to a loss by death. Many of the principles we will discuss can, however, be applied to help those who are grieving because of another type of loss, such as a broken marriage.

Grief which is not dealt with properly can cause us to lose our perspective on life. A friend told me about his mother who mourned the death of her husband so keenly that seventeen years after he died she would cry every time he was mentioned. My friend's wife told her husband, "Honey, I love you very much, but I will never grieve for you for seventeen years!"

Edna St. Vincent Millay expressed the type of hopelessness that many feel in facing a loss. In her poem "Lament," she wrote:

> Life must go on,
> and the dead be forgotten;
> Life must go on,
> Though good men die;
> Anne, eat your breakfast;
> Dan, take your medicine;
> Life must go on;
> I forget just why.

Jesus was no stranger to grief. Isaiah 53:3, 4 foretold that Christ would be "despised and forsaken of men, a man of sorrows, and acquainted with grief" (NASB).

Happiness is a choice, but grief is a certainty. When Jacob thought that Joseph had been torn apart by wild beasts, the Bible says he "tore his clothes and mourned for his son many days." When King David heard that his son had been killed, he expressed his grief in words which have echoed throughout the ages: "O my son Absalom, my son, my son Absalom! would God I had died for thee, O Absalom, my son, my son!" (2 Samuel 18:33 KJV).

When death separates us from someone we love there is a time when we think no one has suffered as we have. But grief is universal. The method of handling grief is personal and vital.

The Emotions of Grief

Guilt is a gripping force that comes when a loved one dies. It's easy to begin the chorus of "if only's" sung to ourselves or someone else. "If only the paramedics hadn't been so slow." "If only I had been there, I could have done something." "If only I hadn't given him that car." "If only I had spent more time with her and told her how much I cared."

There are two kinds of guilt: real and false. Sometimes they are so entwined that we don't know which one we are experiencing. Real guilt comes when we feel or know that we have disobeyed God's commandments or transgressed His standards. False guilt is one of the normal emotions of grief, when someone is feeling guilty for something over which he had no control.

Velma Barfield, the woman executed for the crimes she committed, knew and experienced real guilt. King David must have suffered from real guilt after he had ordered the murder of Uriah, Bathsheba's husband. He cried, "For I know my transgressions, and my sin is always before me" (Psalm 51:3).

We are all imperfect human beings, with imperfect relationships. Nobody's love for friends or family is perfect. The less perfect that love, the more necessary it may seem to those who survive to ritualize grief. Elaborate caskets and burials, beyond the means of the family, may be a way to "atone" for feelings of guilt. However, I don't want to criticize funeral practices; I believe they need to be a matter of personal and thoughtful choice for each family.

Sometimes guilt comes as a result of felt relief when someone who has endured a prolonged illness finally dies. We may say, "We're thankful he's out of his pain." Then afterward guilt creeps in because of such thankfulness.

When neglect or hate have become a part of a relationship, the death of the person who has generated those feelings may result in self-inflicted grief by the survivor. I was told of a young man who had lost both his mother and father as a child. The young man was raised by an aunt who was indifferent to him. He was visited only occasionally by an older brother, who also neglected him. The young man died when he was only twenty-one, and suddenly the aunt and the brother cried foul play against the doctors, demanded retribution from everyone who had been associated with their relative, and mourned loudly and vocally. Guilt as a result of previous neglect was disguised as grief.

The pain of grief often causes people to become resentful, blaming, or condemning toward others for things they did or did not do. Remember what Martha said to Jesus when Lazarus died? She said, "Lord, if you had been here, my brother would not have died" (John 11:32). I wonder if she later wished she had never said those words when Jesus brought Lazarus out of his tomb.

Christians are not immune to guilt feelings. However, they have an advantage over the nonbeliever because of God's grace and forgiveness. The Lord tells us to confess our sins and He will forgive them. Guilt, real or false, is a burden too heavy to carry. Confession brings forgiveness and forgiveness brings freedom.

Some of the most healing words in any language are, "I'm sorry. Will you forgive me?" How much more we need that confession to our Father in heaven, in order to have a spirit which is unbound by stifling self-accusations.

If God willingly forgives us, we must be willing to forgive ourselves.

Grief also quenches the normal zest for living. "I just don't feel like doing anything." In his heart-wrenching book, *A Severe Mercy*, Sheldon Vanauken wrote after his young wife died, "How could things go on when the world had come to an end? How could things—how could I—go on in this void? How could one person, not very big, leave an emptiness that was galaxy-wide?"[1]

After a personal loss people think that nothing looks the same. Food loses its flavor, music seems hollow, and nothing satisfies. Tears come at strange times, often for no apparent reason. The bereaved person may see someone walking down the street who looks like the person who died, and pain comes without warning.

Another emotion of grief is anger. One woman told how she went into the ladies' room at a gathering of Christian women and tried to speak compassionately to someone whose husband had recently died. The young widow shocked the bystanders when she bitterly retorted, "Why did he do this to me? I have two children to raise, we'll probably have to move and find a cheaper place to live. He died and left me in a mess." She was venting feelings that many others have suppressed. Later she may have regretted that tongue-lashing of her deceased husband, but she expressed a common emotion that many have felt.

When a mourner cannot express anger toward the deceased, he or she may look for another scapegoat. In grief, people tend to become critical of others who are continuing life as usual. Blame the doctor, the nurse, the hospital, relatives . . . find someone to blame! Why not blame God? These feelings aren't new. David cried out, "Why are you downcast, O my soul? Why so disturbed within me? . . . I say to God my Rock, 'Why have you forgotten me?'" (Psalm 42:5, 9).

Jesus didn't reason or argue with Martha when she accused Him of neglect. He patiently understood. If we are on the receiving end of anger, we should not take it personally. Wait until the person has had time to stabilize, and then we may be able to discuss it.

Interwoven with the emotions of grief there is a resistance to returning to normal activities. Nothing seems to matter. The closer the grieving person was to the one who died, the more difficult it is to see life in anything but tones of gray. The griever resents those who want him to pick up the pieces and go on as if life had not collapsed. Friends seem callous and thoughtless.

Christians are not stoics like the Greeks of ancient times. The Scriptures see grief as a normal part of the life process. Out of grief often comes depression. Depression is like a dark day when the clouds block out the sun and we say it isn't shining. When someone says he's "in the pits" it is a very appropriate description.

Groping through your own grief is an emotional, physical, and spiritual effort. Faith gives us the power to pass through grief, not avoid it.

The Sun Is Shining . . . Somewhere

We cannot give pat answers or "three easy steps to work through your personal grief." A friend sent us some quotes from W. Graham Scroggie, words which had helped her cope with the loss of her mother. "Let grief do its work. Tramp every inch of the sorrowful way. Drink every drop of the bitter cup. Draw from memory and hope all that they can offer. To see the things our loved ones have left behind will give us daily pain—the clothes they wore, the letters they wrote, the books they read, the chairs in which they sat, the music they loved, the hymns they sang, the walks they took, the games they played, their seat in church, and much beside—but what would we be without these reminders? Would we like quickly to break with the past in order to assuage grief? Those who truly love will say that they have found in sorrow a new joy, a joy which only the broken-hearted can know."

Today we are so health-conscious, and yet when it comes to the sickness of grief, we entertain many misconceptions. First of all, to be emotionally healthy, we should be encouraged to grieve. I believe God gave us tear glands for a good reason and we should not be embarrassed to use them, though mine don't work, even though I have emotions that would make normal tear glands shed tears. It's too bad that courage and tears are seen as opposites. Men, especially, should not see tears as a sign of weakness. In the Old Testament stout-hearted men "lifted up their voice, and wept" (Job 2:12 KJV). Tears were not considered unmanly. David wept over the death of Saul (2 Samuel 1:12); King Jehoash wept as the prophet Elisha's death approached (2 Kings 13:14).

If someone is embarrassed over tears in public, he should feel free to cry it out in privacy. The psalmist said, "My tears have been my food day and night" (Psalm 42:3).

Without an emotional outlet, trying to "keep up appearances" and demonstrate strength, a person may be inflicting great physical harm. In a book called *Good Grief* Granger Westberg said, "As a clergyman in a medical center, where I have worked closely with doctors and their patients for many years, I have slowly become aware of the fact that many of the patients I see are ill because of some unresolved grief situation. Usually the patient first went to see the doctor with a physical complaint. In an increasing number of cases these people tell me about some great loss they have sustained during the past months or year or two. As we talk, it is clear they have not yet worked through some of the central problems related to that loss. I see this so often that I cannot help drawing the conclusion that there is a stronger relationship than we have ever thought between illness and the way in which a person handles a great loss."[2]

Chaplain Phil Manly at the USC Medical Center says there is great evidence that a fourth of all patients hospitalized are there because of unresolved grief in their lives. The Rev. Jack Black has said that when a person breaks down and cries over the loss of a loved one, "that person is behaving and responding as a human being. Crying at the loss of a loved one is a demonstration of love, not weakness. Expressing grief is a witness of our humanity, not an absence of bravery."

Physically, one of the frightening symptoms of grief is the feeling of tightness in the throat. One woman said, "I just can't eat. Everything sticks in my throat." Later she was heard to remark, "The only good thing to come out of my husband's death is that I lost the weight I have been trying to lose for years. I wish he could see me now." A friend remarked, "I think he can, Sally."

Others may experience a shortness of breath, or an empty feeling in the abdomen. One authority on grief said there is "a rather vague misery that we feel everywhere at once and nowhere in particular."

None of these reactions is abnormal. Grievers in this stage should endeavor to take good care of their bodies, eating a proper diet, getting adequate rest, and trying to have a good mental attitude—even if they don't particularly feel like it.

Panic is another emotion that may confront the griever. "I can't think of anything else . . . I think I'm losing my mind." By dwelling on morbid fears and anxieties, the grief-stricken person does, in fact, lose the ability to concentrate, which only intensifies the panic. Panic, in turn, creates a sort of emotional paralysis.

Frankly, I don't know how anyone overcomes the deep, agonizing emotions of the loss of someone very near and dear without the sustaining hand of God. We can help ourselves through periods of grief or panic or fear by believing His promises. He has told us He will be with us always and never leave us or forsake us (Hebrews 13:5). We are told to give Him all of our cares and concerns.

The prophet Micah said, "Though I sit in darkness, the Lord will be my light " (7:8).

A Christian has access to that light. One woman who was grieving over the death of her child, told about claiming a simple verse and repeating it under every circumstance. When she thought she didn't have the strength to get supper she said, "I can do everything through him who gives me strength" (Philippians 4:13). When she needed to be with other people, but wanted to isolate herself in her room, she would open the door and repeat, "I can do all things through Christ." Those words, she said, became her life's verse. They have helped her through many crises since then.

Best of all, there is ultimate and justifiable hope for the Christian. A griever knows when he or she is reaching the reconstruction stage of the grief process when, little by little, hope becomes more of a reality. The time between periods of extreme grief grow longer. The memories become sweeter and less painful. Laughter is genuine, instead of forced. Great verses of hope leap out of the Bible to bring peace and even joy.

"We believe that Jesus died and rose again and so we believe that God will bring with Jesus those who have fallen asleep in him" (1 Thessalonians 4:14). We can rest in the assurance that we will be reunited with our loved ones at the resurrection, as well as being with our Lord and Savior.

"Therefore we are always confident and know that as long as we are at home in the body we are away from the Lord" (2 Corinthians 5:6).

There is no greater comfort than that offered by the promises the God of the universe gives to us. However, anyone who goes through any intense grief experience is never quite the same afterward. He becomes either stronger or weaker, and ultimately he chooses which it will be.

In today's society we feel a sense of urgency to finish one project and move on quickly to another. Most of us don't realize that it takes time to work through losses. The days of mourning and black armbands are ancient history. One of the last prominent personalities to wear the black armband was President Franklin Delano Roosevelt, at the death of his mother. But today we get the impression that any evidence of grief is out of place. Only the one who is grieving knows how long or how severe it may be. No two people are alike and no two grief situations are identical.

Those best prepared for grief are men and women with a deep faith who accepted and trusted God's promises before they had need to claim them. They nurtured their faith by reading and believing the Bible, by observing others in situations of grief, and by building spiritual strength when the sun was yet shining. Someone observed that we tend to buy umbrellas after it starts to rain. How much better to have the umbrella at hand *before* we need it.

But we need help from friends, too, and we must be willing to be receivers of love and hope as well as givers. As we have been comforted, we will know how to comfort. "Praise be to the God and Father of our Lord Jesus

Christ, the Father of compassion and the God of all comfort, who comforts us in all our troubles, so that we can comfort those in any trouble with the comfort we ourselves have received from God" (2 Corinthians 1:3, 4).

The story is told of the rich old widow who acted in a strange manner after the death of her musician husband. Twenty years after he died, she still kept his music studio just as he left it. She locked the keyboard of his piano and did not allow anyone to play it or enter the room. Every day she stood in the doorway of that room, reliving memories and dwelling on the past.

Very likely she had no one to stand by her and help her through the grieving process when her husband died. How badly she needed people to care enough to be there to love and understand, and to help her resume life on her own.

Comfort, O Comfort My People

My wife says that the ones who comforted her mother the most after her father died were the widows who came to the house, put their arms around Mother Bell, and wept with her. They didn't need to say a thing.

But how can we have a ministry of comfort if we have never experienced deep sorrow ourselves? What could we say to the girl whose mother, father, brother, and grandmother were all killed in an automobile accident? What comfort could we offer the parents who have spent two years with a dying child? How could we understand the emotions of a mother and father whose only daughter was a victim of rape-murder by the Hillside Strangler? They are beyond our ability to understand.

173

And yet God does not suggest, He commands us to "Comfort my people" (Isaiah 40:1). However, allow me to make some general observations and suggestions for those who want to obey that command and be a source of support and comfort for the grief-stricken.

The first suggestion is to ask God to give us a tender heart. David asked the Lord, "Create in me a pure heart" (Psalm 51:10). We could add, an understanding heart, an aching heart, a considerate heart. "Finally, all of you, live in harmony with one another; be sympathetic, love as brothers, be compassionate and humble" (1 Peter 3:8). It was told that St. Patrick had this prayer inscribed on his breastplate:

> God be in my head,
>   And in my understanding;
> God be in my eyes,
>   And in my looking;
> God be in my mouth,
>   And in my speaking;
> God be in my heart,
>   And in my thinking;
> God be at mine end,
>   And at my departing.

Sometimes well-meaning Christians will approach a mourner with long scriptures, a series of small sermons, or pious speeches. An example of this took place at the home of a young couple whose baby had just died in that mysterious manner called "crib death." Friends and relatives gathered at their home. One young man, an unmarried seminary student, began to recite all of the recently learned verses of triumph and assurance. His anxiety to repeat all the right phrases, though essentially well-intentioned, was as irritating as a fingernail scraping on a blackboard. One by one, people walked out of the room, leaving only the mourning parents to endure the insensitive seminarian's preaching.

Second, use the gift of listening. Somehow this is very difficult for all of us. We talk, many times, because we think we need to say something. Listening is hard. The sound of our own voices may be therapy for us, but it is not necessarily healing for the wounded griever. During a time of shock people need to repeat their story over and over again. You may think they would grow weary of giving details, or telling what happened, but that isn't the case at all.

A woman told me about her Bible teacher who came to her home after a loved one had died. She expected him to offer some profound truths, to quote Scripture, or to tell stories from the Bible. Instead, he sat on the couch as people came and went. While food was served and removed, and long after everyone was gone, he remained on the couch. Exhausted from the strain, she sat down beside him, and he said, "Tell me how you feel." Years later the woman recalled that one of the people who made the most profound impressions upon her during her stage of grief and shock was that quiet Bible teacher.

It often takes discipline to listen to the same events repeated over and over again. But by listening, we show we love. Remember how God shows His love for us by listening to the cries of our hearts.

In his book, *Comforting Those Who Grieve,* Doug Manning said, "A good listener becomes a walking, touching, personal, intensive care unit. That is what I want to be."[3]

Third, we shouldn't be shocked by whatever the grief-stricken person may say. Death can be a nightmare, and while visitors are there, life and reality may be distorted. A perfectly rational person may say irrational things. One man returned to his home from the hospital where his daughter had died, and saw his best friend sitting in his kitchen, wearing a worn sweater the friend had taken from the closet. The distraught father snapped at his friend, "Why are you wearing that? It's my fishing sweater."

The understanding friend took off the sweater without a word. Did the father make an issue over a trivial matter? Of course he did, but in later years he remembered every detail of that night and thanked his friend for being there when he needed him.

Fourth, let the bereaved one decide if he or she wants Bible reading or prayer. "Would you like to have me pray with you?" is a simple request. But keep it simple and short, for a mind in agony cannot grasp lengthy prayers that circle the globe.

Fifth, anticipate needs without being told. Be the one who asks, "May I answer the phone for you?" Or "I would like to drive you to the funeral home to make the arrangements." Or, "Don't worry about anything in the kitchen, I'll handle it."

One of the worst things to say is, "Call me if you need anything."

Finally, don't stop being a comforter when the wounds seem to be healed. A wedding anniversary, a birthday, holidays, the anniversary of a death, these are hard times to grope through. Remembering those times with an invitation to dinner, a phone call, or a little note, will provide thoughtful comfort.

One loving Christian couple called or sent flowers on the anniversary of the death of their friend's son, every year for several years. They showed their love by not forgetting.

Hope . . . the Most Important Ingredient

Even in the midst of grieving, the mourner sooner or later begins to see little glimmers of hope. First an hour will go by when he does not think of his loss, then a few hours, then a day. He has a good night's sleep for the first time. A meal tastes good. Slowly, reconstruction begins.

For believers in Jesus Christ, verses of hope seem to appear in the Bible, verses they had previously passed over. Passages they have read many times before suddenly stand out with new clarity, with new, deeper meanings. A daughter called her grieving mother long-distance and said, just as if no one had ever discovered this verse before, "Listen, Mom, to what Romans 14:8 says, 'For if we live, we live for the Lord, or if we die, we die for the Lord; therefore whether we live or die, we are the Lord's.' Isn't that great?"

One of the reasons I am writing this book is my gratefulness for the fact that my mother, and others like her, taught me the truth of the verse, "For to me, to live is Christ and to die is gain" (Philippians 1:21).

The Bible says we have a God of hope. In the Scripture we find our hope. Having faith and hope does not mean that we bypass grief, but we can work through it and be strengthened by the experience.

At the beginning of the book we spoke of death as being an enemy. Its companion, grief, does not need to be an enemy, but a process of life through which we can have a closer relationship with Jesus Christ, a stronger bond with other believers, and a greater outreach to others.

Learning How to Live, and Die

During the first few years of my life I lived in a frame farmhouse near Charlotte, North Carolina. When I was about nine years old we moved to our new red brick home, built for $9,000, a roomy, rambling house filled with laughter, books, the smells of cooking and canning, and most of all, an atmosphere of love. That wonderful house reminds me of the proverb, "By wisdom a house is built, and through understanding it is established; through knowledge its rooms are filled with rare and beautiful treasures" (Proverbs 24:3, 4).

My father, Frank Graham, was a farmer whose strength and integrity made him admired, and sometimes feared, by the farmhands and us children. I can still remember the sting of his belt when I had carried some prank to the edge of disobedience. He did not, in my memory, ever punish in anger or desperation, but it pained my mother, nevertheless, and she wrote in later years, "More than once I wiped tears from my eyes and turned my head so the children wouldn't see, but I always stood behind my husband when he administered discipline."[4]

And this country boy certainly needed and deserved the discipline.

My mother, Morrow Coffey Graham, was country bred and country raised. A picture of her at eighteen showed a beautiful young woman, with a Gibson Girl hairdo, an enviable figure, a tiny waist, and a shy smile. She was one of the most beautiful women I have ever known, and she instilled in me a love for the Bible, even when it didn't seem to interest me. She began to read to my brother and sisters from devotionals and many times I thought them extremely boring. However, I listened, probably fidgeting and gazing out the window or cracking my knuckles. My mother told how one day she took me to the family doctor and said, "Billy Frank has too much energy. He never slows down." I've sometimes wondered if she sought advice because of my excess activity or because I simply wore her out.

Mother was a very busy woman with four children and her duties as a farmer's wife. The day I was born she spent much of the afternoon picking beans and then stood in the kitchen, stringing them to prepare for canning. I still remember all the rows of canned fruit and vegetables she lined up on the shelves. She would have at least five hundred jars in the pantry after the canning season, or she wouldn't think it was enough.

Most of all, she loved the Bible. When I was in my teens she and my father were attending a Brethren Bible class and fervently studied their Scofield Bibles. She began to order Christian books from a New York mail order house, becoming an avid reader. There were always good books lying around the house for us to read.

Mother prepared me for the lovely woman who was to become my wife. One letter I wrote said, "The reason I like Ruth so much is that she looks and reminds me of you." Mother told me later that when she finally met Ruth she was so touched, for she felt that Ruth was far above her.

My father and mother influenced and helped direct

me toward the Lord. Although the testimony of my mother's life helped mold me and taught me how to live, the testimony of her last years and her death gave me insight into how to die.

She lived in our family home until the end of her life and ministered with her wonderful spirit.

We rarely had family prayers when I was young— only when I was about fourteen or fifteen did we begin. She wrote, "None of us will ever forget the time when we knelt to pray without my husband there beside us. Mr. Graham (she was very formal in referring to him) was struck in the face by a piece of wood flying from a saw. He hovered between life and death for two days. I remember going up to our bedroom and just laying hold of the Lord. I know I groaned as I pleaded with God to restore my husband to us, once again in perfect health. We needed him so!"[5]

My father did live many years after that life-threatening time; he died in 1962 and my mother lost her beloved husband of forty-six years. Although her life as a wife and mother was productive, the following nineteen years were not lost in sorrowing or useless activity. She was a beautiful example of how Christians should serve the Lord in their latter years. She wrote, "Since the children have married and gone their separate ways, and since my husband's death, I have found myself with more time to devote to prayer. I pray without ceasing for Billy and the tremendous responsibility that God has given to him; but also for my other children, my grandchildren and great-grandchildren, and for worldwide needs."[6]

What comfort it was for me to know that no matter where I was in the world, my mother was praying for me.

The Tender Heart

An eminent psychiatrist said that the chief duty of a human being is to endure life. In contrast, the Westminster Shorter Catechism says, "Man's chief end is to glorify God, and to enjoy Him forever." My mother did just that.

The last two years my mother lived she was cared for by a wonderful Christian woman, Rose Adams. Rose often said that she had a seminary course, living with Mother, and I can believe it. Mother could quote and remember Scriptures and apply them to everyday living better than most ministers. She never had formal training in a Bible college, but said she learned as the Bible says, "For it is: do and do, do and do, rule on rule, rule on rule; a little here, a little there" (Isaiah 28:10). Put all of these bits of learning together and you have a woman whose knowledge touched an untold number of lives.

She was one of my greatest encouragers. The first sermon she ever heard me preach was in an old synagogue, about forty miles from Charlotte. I was home from Bible school for the Christmas holidays and my parents drove me to the service. Mother said later she was so nervous for me that she was wet with cold perspiration. She never remembered what I said that day, but she thought I was very loud. She was right.

While I was in college Mother and Father prayed every day for me and claimed the verse: "Study to shew thyself approved unto God, a workman that needeth not to be ashamed, rightly dividing the word of truth" (2 Timothy 2:15 KJV).

Mother always told me to preach the gospel, and keep it simple. Two weeks before she went to be with the Lord she admonished me with the same words. I said,

"Mother, I'm going to preach His birth, death, and resurrection. I'll preach it until Jesus comes."

She squeezed my hand and said, "I believe it."

What a blessing it is for parents to believe in their children.

As I remembered my mother's last years, and heard from Rose Adams of the thoughts that she shared, I realized that other lives could be blessed by her example.

At one time it was thought that Mother would have to have her leg amputated. When the infection finally cleared and she was sent home from the hospital, she said, "God never uses a person's life until first he has been broken." She was no stranger to mental and physical suffering. She endured pain, but enjoyed life. She said the Lord had dealt with her through heartaches, but said, "God doesn't comfort us to make us comfortable, but to make us comforters."

Rose, a fun-loving, ebullient woman, with a laugh as big as her heart, came to stay with Mother on a full-time basis the last two years of her life. When Rose's husband died, Mother wrote her this note:

Dear Precious One,
When this storm shall pass, the brightness for which He is preparing you will appear unclouded, and it shall be Himself.

Rose and Mother had a routine for their devotions each morning. During this time Mother would quote Scripture and give Rose an application. It was the spiritual food that sustained her through the pain and weakness of her last days.

One of the first scriptures my mother taught all her

children was Ecclesiastes 12:1. "Remember now thy Creator in the days of thy youth, while the evil days come not, nor the years draw nigh, when thou shalt say, I have no pleasure in them" (KJV). She told her grandchildren and great-grandchildren the same thing, urging all of us to learn to love God and study the Bible when we were young. She never stopped studying and told her pastor, Dr. Ross Rhoads, "I just want to study more and more and do what the Bible says." He commented, "Isn't it something . . . here she is eighty-nine years old and the most perfect person I know living by the Word, and yet she says she wants to study more and more."

Rose Adams told us how Mother would say a verse, in that gentle, expressive manner of hers, and then give an illustration of what it meant to her. These gems were not lost, since Rose recorded them in the margin of *Streams in the Desert* or wrote them in her journal. Here are some of her thoughts shortly before she died.

An Understanding Heart

"For I reckon that the sufferings of this present time are not worthy to be compared with the glory which shall be revealed in us" (Romans 8:18 KJV).

Mother commented, "When God afflicts us He hews a rugged stone. It must be shaped, or else we will be thrown aside, useless. What comforts me is this precious thought: we are being shaped into stones for His heavenly temple. To be made like Him is the very object of our earthly existence. He is the shaper and carpenter of the heavenly temple. He must work us into shape. Our part is to be still in His dear hand. Every vexation is a little chip. We must not be in a hurry to go out of the quarry, for there is a certain place for each stone. We must wait until the building is ready for that stone."

"The angel of the Lord encampeth round about them that fear him, and delivereth them" (Psalm 34:7 KJV).

She was very weak the day she read that verse, but said to Rose, "I always wanted to grow old gracefully and have a sweet spirit . . . I don't want to complain, but sometimes I think Satan is trying to use my suffering to force me to complain. But the Lord has given me such great promise to send an angel to surround me."

From the time when she finally quit struggling with her weakness she developed a certain serenity and a peace. She said, "Do not be afraid to enter the cloud which is settling down on your life, for God is in it. The other side is radiant with His glory. If we are to wear a crown we must first bear a cross. We all have a Gethsemane . . . Jesus did." Mother couldn't understand people who taught that if you are filled with the Spirit and walk with the Lord you won't suffer. She believed that was a cruel teaching.

Was she afraid to die? Not really. And yet she told Rose she was afraid of being left alone in her last moments. She had not been with my father when he went to be with the Lord and always regretted her absence. Rose promised to be with her, and she kept that promise.

The Last Mile

After a series of minor strokes Mother would become confused at times. When she was lucid she told Rose, "If I get so I don't know what I'm doing, you make sure that I'm fixed . . . Put a little color on my face, but don't make me look worldly. I just don't want the children to see me look poorly."

Gracious to the last, this dear lady wanted to be attractive for us. We always thought she was beautiful, and age only enhanced her charm.

She believed the only reason the Lord was delaying His coming for her was so she could pray for others. "That's about all I'm able to do now," she would say. But what an amazing ministry that was. Until the very last few months, whenever she heard of someone in need she would have Rose write a little note and send a few dollars, as had been her habit for so many years. One of her greatest joys was to listen to the records of George Beverly Shea. She played them almost every day and especially loved it when he sang "Be Still My Soul," "He Will Give His Angels Charge Over Thee," and "Amazing Grace."

In the last months she began to dread seeing the approach of evening. "Nights are so long," she would tell Rose in her fading voice. But she quoted Revelation 22:5 which speaks about heaven and says, "And there shall be no night there; and they need no candle, neither light of the sun; for the Lord God giveth them light: and they shall reign for ever and ever" (KJV).

In May of 1981 she said, "Rose, I feel it won't be long until the Lord takes me home. I don't want any mourning or sad spirits. It says in Acts 27:22, 'And now I exhort you to be of good cheer: for there shall be no loss of any man's life among you, but of the ship'" (KJV).

In June of 1981 I was holding a crusade in Baltimore. I called every day to see how Mother was doing and Rose said she listened to the tapes of the hymns Ruth had recorded a few years before for her mother.

My wife knew the comfort in music and compiled some of the great old songs into a cassette which was called "Looking Homeward." Ruth's mother had a tape recorder on her bed and would switch it on and off to hear the inspiring music. A few years later we had those tapes sent to our television audience and received one of the largest responses to any book or tape we ever gave away. The comfort our mothers found resulted in comfort for many thousands.

On June 15 I called from France and Rose said Mother had given her the scripture for the day, Colossians 1:9: "For this cause we also, since the day we heard it, do not cease to pray for you, and to desire that ye might be filled with the knowledge of his will in all wisdom and spiritual understanding" (KJV).

While I was concerned about my dear mother, thousands of miles away on a bed of weakness and pain, she had a verse of encouragement for me. What would the world be like if there were more mothers like her? She didn't make great speeches or write clever books. She didn't have any great causes to espouse, except the cause of Jesus Christ. She didn't have university degrees, nor was she mentioned in society columns. But she knew how to pray.

The Lord seems to prepare His children for their homecoming in most unique ways. Toward the end of July Mother constantly talked about going to heaven. Rose asked her if she could come to her mansion in heaven and work for her because she thought her house would be very small and she wouldn't have much to do, but Mother Graham's would be so large she'd need help.

One morning when she awoke, she told Rose there

was a man at the foot of her bed. She wanted to know who he was.

Rose asked her if he looked like a good man.

"Oh yes, he has a very kind face."

"Maybe he's your guardian angel."

Mother then asked, "Who is that woman who comes in with you?"

This time Rose was startled. "There hasn't been anyone with me," she said.

"Oh, but for the last two weeks every time you came in the room there's been someone with you. She just stands beside you. She must be your guardian angel. Now, get me ready for church."

The beginning of August, 1981, Mother awoke around midnight and called to Rose, who was sleeping nearby on a pallet in the living room. "Rose, are all the children on the train?"

Rose told her everything was all right and the children were on the train. She would quiet down for a time and then try to lift herself up from the bed and call again, "Rose, are all of the children on the train?"

"Don't you worry, Mother Graham, they're all there," she said. Rose went back to bed, but soon Mother became more persistent.

"Rose, please check and see if all the children are on the train." Somehow she seemed to know she was going somewhere and wanted to be certain her children were going with her. We believe she was seeking assurance that all of her family were saved.

On August 8, my brother, Melvin, T. W. Wilson, and I went to see her. She wanted us to tell Ruth and Mary Helen (T. W.'s wife) how much she loved them. She was always so proud of the wives of our team, whose unselfish loyalty meant so much to all of us, particularly when we had to be gone so much. She urged us to continue preaching the gospel and to be faithful in winning the lost.

The next day she was in a semicoma, but woke early in the morning, long enough to announce very loudly. "No payment, no pain, no sickness, no death . . . O what a beautiful day!"

Rose hurried to her bedside, wondering why she had spoken so forcefully when she had been so weak, and said, "Mother Graham, are you all right?"

She said, "Am I in a coma yet?"

"No, Ma'am."

"Am I dead yet? Are we in heaven yet?"

"No, Ma'am," Rose answered, "you're not in heaven 'cause I'm still with you."

"Oh well," sighed Mother, "it's a beautiful day, anyhow."

When she was too weak to speak, she seemed to be moaning and trying to sing a little tune. Rose leaned down close to her mouth and she picked out the words, "Face to face." Then she said, "Psalm . . . 1 . . . 4" and would doze off.

Rose tried to figure out what she was trying to say, and then remembered Psalm 149:5 was underlined in her Bible. It says, "Let the saints be joyful in glory: let them sing aloud upon their beds" (KJV). She was trying to sing, but couldn't voice the words; however, her habit of Bible memorization recalled the proper verse at a time when she needed it.

The morning she went to be with the Lord she kept reaching up . . . she tried to say something about hand,

and Rose didn't know what she wanted. Perhaps, Rose thought, she is trying to say a verse of Scripture, but couldn't get the words out.

"Mother Graham, are you trying to say, 'Father, into Thy hands I commend my spirit'?"

Her hand dropped and a smile came upon her lips. She looked peaceful all day, and once when Rose was about to leave the room, she seemed to yawn. Rose put her arms around her and Mother went to be with her precious Lord.

9

IS YOUR HOUSE

IN ORDER?

"How do we prepare for that last day? Before we embark on our final trip, have we left an earthly home in a state of chaos or a condition of order?"

Set thine house in order; for thou shalt die, and not live.

2 Kings 20:1 KJV

Going through some old newspaper clippings that Ruth had saved, we found one dated May 5, 1957, entitled "You must prepare for that last day." As I began to reminisce about what was happening in our lives thirty years ago, the humor and irony of that article hit me.

On May 15, 1957, we began the New York Crusade. After we had accepted the challenge to hold those important meetings, it was reported that "This invitation brought upon Graham's head some of the most violent opposition he had ever experienced."[1] I wonder if Ruth thought I was heading for my "last day" in Madison Square Garden?

Incidentally, we were there for sixteen weeks. Only on the second night did we have empty seats; it became our most successful American crusade. At Madison Square Garden we began to put our crusades on national television at prime evening times.

Preparation for the Journey

But how do we prepare for that *last day?* What if the old bedtime rhyme, "If I should die before I wake," becomes a reality? Before we embark on our final trip, have we left an earthly home in a state of chaos or a condition of order?

A young minister said that about once a year he asks his wife, "What if I had just died . . . what would you do?" He doesn't ask her to rehearse grief reactions but to go through the mechanics of saying whom she would call, where important documents are kept, what arrangements she should make with the executor of their estate. This may not be a very enjoyable exercise, but both the husband and the wife say this mock rehearsal gives them a peace of mind and an openness of communication they did not have before they set their "house in order." They are planning in their thirties what many people leave until their seventies. How many heartaches for survivors would be avoided by planning ahead.

The prophet Isaiah delivered a tough message from God to King Hezekiah, "Put your house in order, because you are going to die" (38:1). That crisp command brings into sharp focus a vital, but often neglected, aspect of Christian stewardship. It is the responsibility of every believer while he or she is alive and able to make proper preparations spiritually, as well as fiscally, for the distribution of property and possessions he leaves behind at his death.

The first step in preparation is to accept the fact that we *are* going to die. Unless we are willing to talk openly about this fact, we will never be motivated to follow through on any of the remaining steps.

I have faced death many times and my reactions have not always been the same. Many years ago I had an operation that almost ended me. As a result, a second operation was required to save my life, and before I went into the operating room I called two of my good friends. Ruth was not with me, and I tried to keep from her the seriousness of the situation. She had gone to be with the children. But I gave to these friends instructions for my wife, my family, and my ministry.

During that time, I can remember alternating between complete peace in knowing that I would be with my Lord Jesus Christ, and a fear of leaving my loved ones. Neither emotion predominated, but I seemed to vacillate back and forth. My memory of that time is clouded because of the pain, but I certainly thought I was going to die.

A recent brush with death occurred on an airplane over the Atlantic, when Ruth and I were returning from Europe. It had been an uneventful flight until, suddenly, there was an explosion; the airplane began to vibrate and lose altitude. Dishes flew off trays, people were jolted in their seats, and we thought a bomb was going to finish all of us. There was some comment about turbulence, and we never found out exactly what happened, but we were all immediately aware of our mortality.

We landed safely and thanked the Lord again for giving us a little more time to be doing His work.

I remember a story the late Dr. V. Raymond Edman, former president of Wheaton College, told about his first encounter with death. As a young missionary in Ecuador he contracted typhoid fever while working among the Indians in the Andes Mountains. After several days he was unconscious but, as he described it, fully aware that death was closing in on him. In fact, his friends had bought a coffin for him and helped his wife dye her wedding dress black for the funeral. Dr. Edman said that he experienced the overwhelming love of God and remembered the wonderful assurance that "if our earthly house of this tabernacle were dissolved, we have a building of God, an house not made with hands, eternal in the heavens" (2 Corinthians 5:1 KJV).

In remembering that story, I can't help speculating that Mrs. Edman must have rejoiced that her black wedding dress was never worn.

Author Edward Young wrote that procrastination is the thief of time. Procrastination may also be the thief of our loved ones' sense of security. None of us wants to compound someone else's grief, but many do by their failure to practice good stewardship. Stewardship is more than just giving our tithe to the church or Christian organizations. The faithful Christian steward acknowledges that God owns all he has, and it is his responsibility to manage and dispose of his possessions in a way that is acceptable to the Lord. "Now it is required that those who have been given a trust must prove faithful" (1 Corinthians 4:2).

Stewardship is not just the tithe we give during our lifetime, but a responsibility which continues after our death. We should, as did the young minister and his wife, rehearse in our minds what needs to be done.

It has been said that someone found St. Francis working in his garden and asked him, "What would you

196

do if you knew that you would die in ten minutes?" St. Francis replied, "I'd try to finish this row."

Most of us are not that ready. We might need ten days instead of ten minutes!

Putting Things in Order

After accepting our mortality, the next step is to put our material affairs in order. Dr. Bell taught me a great lesson about that. When I was a very young man, he urged me to make a will. When he, himself, died, his papers were found to be perfectly categorized and numbered in file folders, and there was no confusion about how he wanted his earthly estate to be dispersed.

From that I learned the value of writing down instructions and leaving vital information where it could be found. This includes providing information about where bank books are kept, how insurance papers are filed, and where the key is to your safe deposit box. Our treasures may be laid up in heaven, but those things we leave on earth will mean a great deal more to those we leave behind. Many Christians today seek to include their church and other ministries in their will.

Years ago I read an article by Dr. Edman in the Wheaton College bulletin. It was called, "Facing Death Unafraid," and his description of stewardship made a lasting impression on me. He said, "To the best of my knowledge, all arrangements for the eventuality of death had been made. Just recently Mrs. Edman and I had brought our wills up to date. This was the fourth revision. Conditions had changed since the four boys were little fellows. Furthermore, we had completed a life estate plan with a Christian organization. After much prayer and planning we had sought the counsel and help of those qualified to advise the Lord's people in these matters, for it is our conviction that no matter how large or how modest the estate, plans should be laid so that nothing is wasted."[2]

I have heard so many stories of people who have spent weeks, sometimes months and years, trying to find documents and straighten out the estate of a deceased member of the family. One such story concerns a fine Christian physician who was dying of cancer. Long before his death he knew that the end was certain. He continued with his practice as long as he could, but during the final months of his life was not able to make clear decisions.

His widow believed she had been properly taken care of and would enjoy some degree of financial independence. She had never questioned her husband's arrangements, having depended upon his wisdom to leave his house in order. But within a year the distraught widow found she had been left penniless and in debt. She was forced to sell the family home, take her daughter out of college, and go to work in a menial job. As a society wife of a prominent surgeon, it had never been necessary for her to learn any earning skills, but suddenly she was faced with the need to support herself and her children.

Perhaps there should be more of us who proclaim the practical applications of Isaiah's warning to Hezekiah, "Set your house in order."

Plan Your Own Funeral

Did you make plans for your own wedding? Did you ever have a special party, an anniversary or birthday celebration, where you planned in advance what you would do? Then what's so strange about planning your own funeral?

I have preached at many funerals. It seems to me that those loved ones who have some knowledge of the wishes of the deceased move through the funeral process with less anxiety than those who have no idea what the departed one might have wanted. I remember one sincere request made by President Lyndon Johnson after he retired from public life. I had delivered the invocation at the dedication of the Johnson Library in Austin, Texas, and later LBJ took me to his ranch in the Hill Country. We walked down to the oak trees by the Pedernales River and he said, "Billy, one day you're going to be asked to preach at my funeral. You'll come right here under this tree and I'll be buried right there." And he pointed to the spot. "You'll read the Bible and preach the gospel, and I want you to, but I hope you'll try to tell some of the things I tried to do."

President Johnson and I spoke about the brevity of life, and the fact that someday we will stand before God to give an account. We discussed the resurrection at some length.

Just fifteen minutes after I returned home from President Richard Nixon's second inauguration I heard of Mr. Johnson's death. On January 25, 1973, I preached beneath that old oak tree, as he requested, and the nation watched on television.

Though in many ways he was a rough man, and a complex man, down deep in his heart he loved God. A number of times it had been my privilege to be with him both in Washington and in Texas, and have prayer with him. I can remember seeing him climb out of bed and get down on his knees while I prayed.

So it was with a heart full of love that I told about

the man I knew: his compassion for the underdog, his friendship for children of all races, his strong family life and, most importantly, his faith. My biographer, John Pollock, wrote how I spoke of death, judgment, and the Cross, and said, "Lyndon Johnson understood that . . . for the believer who has been to the Cross, death is no frightful leap in the dark, but is the entrance into a glorious new life . . . . For the believer, the brutal fact of death has been conquered by the historical resurrection of Jesus Christ. For the person who has turned from sin and received Christ as Lord and Savior, death is not the end . . . ."[3]

That is what President Lyndon Johnson wanted me to say.

Why give instructions for your own funeral? Certainly not because you will be concerned about them. You won't attend your own funeral. However, your spouse, your children, your friends and business associates may all be there. The survivors would want to know your wishes. Where will you be buried? Have you left instructions about cremation or a burial plot? What hymns would you want to be sung? Are there any words of assurance you would want to be said to your loved ones and friends? Are there any requests about an open or closed casket?

How often the survivors of the deceased have to struggle with those decisions when they are in no condition to be making such plans, and when it would have been so much easier to have the plans already made and settled.

If we plan our own funeral, we should keep in mind family traditions or customs in the part of the country where we live. For instance, in many places viewing the body is an important part of the grief process which allows the survivors to say farewell to the physical part of the person they loved. It gives a certain finality to the death process.

I remember when Richard Nixon's mother died. I had the privilege of participating in her funeral. I had known his father and mother before I knew him and, as was the custom in that Quaker city of Whittier, California, people filed by to see the open casket. The pastor of the church and I stood there beside the casket, then the Nixon family came in. As the future president looked at his mother he burst into tears. He had a deep love for his mother, and for all his family.

However, for some people the cosmetic attempts upon the deceased are unseemly. It is important to be sensitive to the feelings of others when we make decisions about our own funeral or memorial service.

Personally, Ruth and I know where we will be buried and we have expressed our desires to have a home-going "celebration," not a woeful wake.

Of course, I cannot make definitive statements about planning your own funeral since it is a subject with so many personal applications. However, biblical precedents have been set for us by some of the great Old Testament believers who gave personal burial instructions. Jacob said, "I am about to be gathered to my people. Bury me with my fathers in the cave in the field of Ephron the Hittite . . . ." After he expressed his wishes, the Bible says, he went peacefully. "When Jacob had finished giving instructions to his sons, he drew his feet up into the bed, breathed his last and was gathered to his people" (Genesis 49:29, 33).

"By faith," the writer tells us, "Joseph, when his end

was near . . . gave instructions about his bones"
(Hebrews 11:22).

These two great patriarchs didn't use long-range
planning, but at least they had definite arrangements
which were made known to their kinsmen.

It was reported that President Franklin Delano
Roosevelt left exact instructions concerning his funeral
in a four-page, penciled document addressed to his
eldest son, James. It read, "If I should die while in office,
I want a service of the utmost simplicity held in the East
Room of the White House. There should be no lying in
state, no gun carriage and no hearse. The casket should
be of utmost simplicity in dark wood. The body should
not be embalmed or hermetically sealed. The grave
should not be lined with brick, cement or stones."[4]

Those directions were certainly explicit. There was
only one catch. No one in the Roosevelt family knew this
document existed. It was found in the President's private
safe a few days after he was buried.

It may be wise for us to make arrangements for our
funerals, but our most carefully drawn plans won't do
any good if no one knows where they are!

Planning your own funeral is a gift from you to your
survivors. No one can convey what you wish to leave as a
personal testimony better than you can. Others may ex-
tol your virtues, and ignore your shortcomings, but only
you can tell of your love for the Lord, your appreciation
of your family, and your anticipation of heaven, if those
are your personal beliefs.

Funerals Are for the Living

Every culture has had its ceremonies for meeting
emotional crises. All of the major changes in life, from

birth to adolescence, marriage, and death, have been dignified by rituals. A funeral should be a ritual which meets the social, emotional, and spiritual needs of the survivors.

A newspaper columnist wrote, "Funerals are for the living, not the dead, and I've never attended one that I thought did a good job of comforting the survivors, or really helped them to work through their grief."[5]

On the contrary, I have attended and officiated at many funerals where I felt that the funeral or memorial service was a turning point in the lives of some of those attending. Often, from the witness of the life and death of the deceased, or the statements made by family members, uncommitted men and women have been convicted about their own lives and have been directed to a loving God.

For believers in Jesus Christ, a Christian funeral reaffirms the blessed hope of eternal life and the resurrection. Jesus said, "I tell you the truth, whoever hears my word and believes him who sent me has eternal life and will not be condemned; he has crossed over from death to life" (John 5:24).

When Martha needed comfort about the death of her brother, Lazarus, Jesus said to her, "I am the resurrection and the life. He who believes in me will live, even though he dies; and whoever lives and believes in me will never die. Do you believe this?" (John 11:25).

At a funeral service the bereaved can be drawn closer to the Lord, experiencing His comfort, as Martha did, and as other believers have throughout the ages. The writer who said he had never attended a funeral where survivors were comforted also admitted that he didn't believe in an afterlife and doubted that his spirit would be transformed in a world elsewhere. Such skepticism

only serves to rob the funeral service of anything meaningful. It leaves the bereaved with no hope.

A funeral should provide a time for relatives,
friends, and church family to support the grieving loved
ones and to express concern and sympathy for their loss.
Even if friends never knew the deceased, it is a time to
show their love for the survivors. We honor the dead at
such a service, but we also are provided with a tangible
way of ministering to the bereaved before, during, and
after the funeral.

Years ago, a Christian wrote a letter which she in-
structed to be sent to friends after her memorial service
was held. She was an English teacher at a small Texas
college, and a devout Christian. She said, "All my life-
long study of literature has taught me that when the
writer is great enough, the end is the best part of
the book. I am a volume written by a divine Writer,
and the climax is the best part of the book."

A Christian funeral should be a coronation ceremony, a statement to the world about eternal life.

Do You Need a Will?

Polls show that only about one in every five adults
has made a will. When we see the problems created for
the surviving family members whenever anyone dies
without leaving one, it should convict us with our own
sense of responsibility. Recently I learned of a prominent
business person, head of a large company, who died
without leaving a will. It is difficult to understand how
anyone of that stature could have neglected such an important document; however, it is startling to me to find
out how prevalent this omission really is. Such situations
create needless hardships and heartache for loved ones.

The Lord's work suffers because of this lack of concern on the part of such a great number of Christians.

What is a will? Essentially, it is a legal document that names the people—family members, friends, business associates—as well as the organizations, churches, and charities that you choose to receive your property when you die.

I remember once when Charlie Riggs and I were flying late at night on the west coast of Africa in an old Ghanian Airways DC-3. We ran into a terrible thunderstorm and none of us thought that old plane could possibly survive. People all around us started screaming, and one big, strong Nigerian man sitting beside Charlie began sobbing so loudly everyone on the plane could hear him. Later, I asked Charlie why the Nigerian had been weeping so bitterly and Charlie said the man was sure he was going to die and his body was going to fall into the water where his son could not recover it. Among his people, the son could not inherit anything from the father unless his body was found.

Your estate includes personal property, such as automobiles, stocks, interest in a business, furniture, jewelry, dishes, a stamp collection or books, or other similar personal effects. I suspect my wife would say her most important possessions are her books.

When Dr. Bell, my father-in-law, died, the family went to his closet and found only two suits and one pair of shoes. He had arranged his personal effects impeccably for his departure, but even these few things which he had kept were important to his family.

Your estate also includes real property, which is land and any buildings you own or any improvements that stand on the land.

Who among us can make a will? Generally, anyone

who is eighteen years of age or older can write a will. For it to be valid, you must be of sound mind, which means that you must understand what property you own, about how much it's worth, and to whom you are leaving it.

You may name your own "executor," who is the person, bank, or corporation which will handle your affairs after you die, until your property is distributed in accordance with your will or other legal settlement. The executor collects any money owed to your estate, pays your debts and taxes, and gives the remaining property to the persons or organizations named in the will.

If an executor is not named, the court will appoint someone to settle the affairs of the estate. This may not be the person you would have chosen.

Your will lets you name a guardian for your minor children. This can be important if both parents die at the same time, or if you're a single parent. If you don't name a guardian, it will be up to the court to decide where the children will live and how to spend any money you leave for their care. For anyone with minor children, this fact alone should be reason enough to get a will written now.

A will should generally be drawn up by a lawyer, but under certain conditions you may write your own will. If you have a handwritten, or "holographic" will, the law says that your signature and all important parts of the will must be in your own writing. It should be dated, but witnesses are not required. Not all states accept such handwritten wills, however, so you should be sure it is legal where you live, and if you should move to another state, don't forget to check the laws there.

Some married couples, believing that their goals and desires are the same, want to write a joint will. But lawyers and administrators warn against the perils of this practice, since in a joint will two people say what's to be done with each one's property. If both people agree that their joint will is final, it can't be changed later by the survivor. I know a woman who took the opportunity to change a joint will after the death of her husband. The couple had four children and the husband had left somewhat more money to two of them. When those two found out, a few years later, that their share had been reduced by their mother so that all the children would share equally, they were so upset that they begged, and almost threatened, the other two until they were given some of the money that had originally (and legally) been left to them.

You can imagine what complications might arise if, for instance, the spouse who survives should remarry, or children who are to receive property become irresponsible. Joint wills may sound like a noble statement that both partners are of like mind, but the actual consequences of such a will can be disturbing.

If you die without a will, the court will distribute your property to your relatives in a manner established by law. However, your property cannot go to friends, charities, or churches if you do not leave a will so stating. There can be no special provisions for heirlooms, jewelry, or the family business.

Your will remains in effect until you change it or draft a new one. Many people will be convinced they need a will, have one drawn up, and then let it sit for years without giving it another thought. "Sure, I have a will," they say, confidently. However, since that will was written, children may have grown and married, grandchildren may have been born, tax laws changed, estate size increased, and the original will may have little validity anymore. A review should be made of your will every few years. The court will follow your most recent will.

The law gives you many choices if you make a will, but none at all if you don't.

A Christian's will should be a matter of much prayer and thoughtfulness, including perhaps not only gifts to individuals but to one's church or to other religious organizations. A Christian's will may also contain more than directions on how money and possessions are to be dispersed. It can also be a testimony to those who read it. It can be a lasting memorial to faith in Christ and love for others. Someone said that he could tell better what a man had in his heart by reading his will than by reading his obituary. "For as he thinketh in his heart, so is he" (Proverbs 23:7 KJV).

Many of us who have read and loved the books written by Charles Dickens have thought that he must have been a Christian. Generations of readers have laughed and cried over his *Pickwick Papers, Oliver Twist, David Copperfield,* and *Nicholas Nickleby.* Not a Christmas goes by without many revivals of his great classic, *A Christmas Carol.* But it was not the great books he wrote nor the lengthy eulogy in the *London Times* when he died that will be recorded in eternity, but the inheritance he left in his will. He wrote: "I commit my soul to the mercy of God, through our Lord and Savior Jesus Christ, and I exhort my dear children humbly to try and guide themselves by the teaching of the New Testament."[6]

The best preparation for death is not a list of instructions about our funeral, not an up-to-date will, but an experience with Christ that gives eternal life. " . . . a faith and knowledge resting on the hope of eternal life, which God, who does not lie, promised before the beginning of time" (Titus 1:2).

The hope of eternal life becomes more precious when we increase our knowledge of what that means. Our everyday existence is so centered on what is happening to us on earth that the prospect of eternity may be perceived as overwhelming—even frightening.

What does await us in eternity? Is it a journey into the unknown, or a glorious spiritual pilgrimage to eagerly anticipate?

We will all go on the trip to eternity, and we make the choice of the type of reservations we will have to determine our destiny.

10

WHERE DO I GO

WHEN I DIE?

"Throughout our culture we have been led to the idea that we accept death as the end of life on earth. . . . Time bound as we are and goal oriented to achievements in our lifetime, we find it strange to anticipate heaven."

I consider that our present sufferings are not worth comparing with the glory that will be revealed in us.

Romans 8:18

A ghostly imperial guard of more than seven thousand life-size clay soldiers has been unearthed in mainland China. Archaeologists recently uncovered these massive terra-cotta statues, considered one of the most spectacular finds of the age. The royal army, standing in battle formation to protect the grave of China's first emperor, Shih Huang Ti, was equipped with war chariots and weapons of wood and bronze. Their horses, harnessed in gold and silver, lay in a pit near the tomb. In this amazing discovery, we see death depicted as a battleground. The emperor wanted assurance of protection in the afterworld.

Man's final destination has been pondered throughout the ages. Some have accepted the tradition of their ancestors, others have struggled with conflicting ideas. Buddhists and Hindus believe they will undergo repeated rebirths, transmigrating from existence to existence; there is no beginning and no end of a continuing life; they are reincarnated into other bodies.

The Taoist treats death with indifference; oblivion is a state of non-doing. Islamic belief recognizes seven heavens, places of carnal pleasure and spiritual bliss. American Indian culture speaks of the "Happy Hunting Ground." Most adherents to Judaism believe in a heaven where good deeds done on earth are rewarded.

The Christian has a strong hope of heaven because of what Jesus Christ has done through His death and resurrection. "Praise be to the God and Father of our Lord Jesus Christ! In his great mercy he has given us new birth into a living hope through the resurrection of Jesus Christ from the dead, and into an inheritance that can never perish, spoil or fade—kept in heaven for you" (1 Peter 1:3–4).

At the same time there are many things about heaven we do not know for sure. "Now we see but a poor reflection; then we shall see face to face. Now I know in part; then I shall know fully, even as I am fully known" (1 Corinthians 13:12).

One unknown poet expressed it this way:

> When the holy angels meet us,
> As we go to join their band,
> Shall we know the friends that greet us,
> In the glorious spirit-land?
> Shall we see the same eyes shining
> On us, as in days of yore?
> Shall we feel their dear arms twining

Fondly 'round us as before?
Shall we know each other there?

What Right Have You to Enter Heaven?

Every man and woman who has ever lived will have to answer that question. A woman who had just experienced a death in her family told me she felt such an urgency to share Christ with someone that when a repairman came in to fix the furnace she backed him up against the wall and said, "If that furnace had blown up in your face and you had died, would you know for certain where you would spend eternity?" The repairman was so startled he forgot to leave a bill.

Why do some people believe they have a paid ticket to heaven? They give many answers, but most can be classified within three basic attitudes. The first is, "Just look at what I've done on earth. My record is pretty good, compared to some. I'll be in heaven because I lived such a good life."

That person is in trouble. The Bible says "for all have sinned and fall short of the glory of God" (Romans 3:23). So if we're placing our good deeds on a scale of 1 to 10, even a perfect 10 wouldn't make it. No one can ever live a life that is "good enough." The Bible says, "For whoever keeps the whole law and yet stumbles at just one point is guilty of breaking all of it" (James 2:10).

The second answer might be, "I really don't know, and I'm not sure that I care. I gave it some thought for a while, but there were so many other things that seemed more important."

As mothers say, "Excuses will get you nowhere." The Bible says, "For since the creation of the world

215

God's invisible qualities—his eternal power and divine nature—have been clearly seen, being understood from what has been made, so that men are without excuse" (Romans 1:20).

Only one answer will give a person the certain privilege, the joy, of entering heaven. "Because I have believed in Jesus Christ and accepted Him as my Savior. He is the One sitting at the right hand of God and interceding for me." No one can deny that Christian his entrance into heaven.

The Heidelberg Catechism, originally written in 1563 and used by Christians of many backgrounds, was a favorite of my father-in-law. On his study wall he had the first question and answer of the Heidelberg Catechism framed, which reads, "Q. 1. What is your only comfort, in life and in death? A. That I belong—body and soul, in life and death—not to myself but to my faithful Savior, Jesus Christ, who at the cost of his own blood has fully paid for all my sins and has completely freed me from the dominion of the devil; that he protects me so well that without the will of my Father in heaven not a hair can fall from my head; indeed, that everything must fit his purpose for my salvation. Therefore, by his Holy Spirit, he also assures me of eternal life, and makes me wholeheartedly willing and ready from now on to live for him."

"Who will bring any charge against those whom God has chosen? It is God who justifies. Who is he that condemns? Christ Jesus, who died—more than that, who was raised to life—is at the right hand of God and is also interceding for us" (Romans 8:33, 34).

What a magnificent thought! Jesus is our advocate, our lawyer, pleading our case before God the Father, telling Him that the person being presented for entrance into heaven must be admitted on the basis of God's grace alone, not by any good works or noble deeds done on earth.

Many people are deceived by Satan into thinking that God is a vengeful taskmaster, ready to send to hell all those who offend Him. They can see no hope. True, God does hate sin, but He loves the sinner. Since we are all sinners, our only right for admission to heaven lies in the provision God made for our sins: His Son, Jesus Christ. "For God so loved the world that he gave his one and only Son, that whoever believes in him shall not perish but have eternal life" (John 3:16).

Do We Decide to Go to Hell?

Hell has been cloaked in folklore and disguised in fiction for so long, many people deny the reality of such a place. Some think it is merely a myth. This is understandable. Our minds revolt against ugliness and suffering. However, the concept of hell is not exclusive to the Christian faith.

Centuries before Christ, the Babylonians believed in "The Land of No-Return." The Hebrews wrote about going down to the realm of Sheol, or the place of corruption; the Greeks spoke of the "Unseen Land." Classical Buddhism recognizes seven "hot hells," and the Hindu *Rig Veda* speaks of the deep abyss reserved for false men and faithless women. Islam recognizes seven hells.[1]

Jesus specifically states that nonbelievers will not be able to escape the condemnation of hell (Matthew 23:33). He told His disciples, "Do not be afraid of those who kill the body and after that can do no more. But I will show you whom you should fear: Fear him who, after

217

the killing of the body, has power to throw you into hell" (Luke 12:4, 5).

Probably one of the most graphic descriptions of hell in the Bible is given by Jesus in His parable of the rich man and Lazarus. During his life the rich man refused to help Lazarus, a poor beggar who yearned to eat crumbs which fell from the rich man's table. When the beggar died, he was carried to Abraham's side, which was what we would describe as heaven. The rich man was sent to hell and was in torment. Jesus did not imply that having wealth means being doomed to hell, nor did he say that being poor guarantees anyone the right to heaven. However, it is a graphic description of the unbeliever's suffering apart from God.

According to the parable, the rich man looked up and saw Abraham, with the beggar by his side. He spoke through cracked, parched lips and pleaded for Abraham to ask Lazarus to dip his finger in some water and bring it to him to cool his tongue. "I am in agony in this fire," he cried.

But Abraham said there was a great chasm between the two worlds and it was "fixed," or permanent. No person on one side could cross over to the other. In other words, the one in hell had been given a choice of direction during his life on earth, and now he had to suffer the consequences of his decision to live for himself instead of for God. There was no second chance.

Hell: A Controversial Subject

I am continually asked, "What about hell?" or "Is there fire in hell?" and similar questions. I cannot ignore this unpopular subject, although it makes people uncomfortable and anxious. It is probably the hardest of all Christian teachings to accept.

Some teach "universalism"—that eventually everybody will be saved and the God of love will never send anyone to hell. They believe the words "eternal" or "everlasting" do not actually mean forever. However, the same word which speaks of eternal banishment from God is also used for the eternity of heaven.

Others teach that those who refuse to accept Jesus Christ as Savior are simply annihilated, they no longer exist. I've searched the Bible and have never found convincing evidence to support this view. The Bible teaches whether we are saved or lost, there is an everlasting existence of the soul.

Some believe God gives a second chance. But the Bible says, "Now is the day of salvation" (2 Corinthians 6:2). At our crusades I invite people to accept Christ right then, for we do not know when we will pass into eternity.

The Bible teaches there is hell for every person who willingly and knowingly rejects Christ as Lord and Savior. Many passages could be quoted to support that fact.

"But anyone who says, 'you fool!' will be in danger of the fire of hell" (Matthew 5:22).

"The Son of Man will send out his angels, and they will weed out of his kingdom everything that causes sin and all who do evil. They will throw them into the fiery furnace, where there will be weeping and gnashing of teeth" (Matthew 13:41, 42).

"Then death and Hades were thrown into the lake of fire. The lake of fire is the second death. If anyone's name was not found written in the book of life, he was thrown into the lake of fire" (Revelation 20:14, 15).

In the Sermon on the Mount, Jesus said, "It is better for you to lose one part of your body than for your whole body to be thrown into hell" (Matthew 5:29).

Will a loving God send a man to hell? The answer from Jesus and the teachings of the Bible is, clearly, "Yes!" He does not send man willingly, but man condemns himself to eternal hell because in his blindness, stubbornness, egotism, and love of sinful pleasure, he refuses God's way of salvation and the hope of eternal life with Him.

Suppose a person is sick and goes to a doctor. The doctor diagnoses the problem and prescribes medicine. However, the advice is ignored and in a few days the person stumbles back into the doctor's office and says, "It's your fault that I'm worse. Do something."

God has prescribed the remedy for the spiritual sickness of the human race. The solution is personal faith and commitment to Jesus Christ. Since the remedy is to be born again, if we deliberately refuse it, we must suffer the horrible consequences.

Yes, there is an alternative to heaven. No matter what your conception of it may be, we know it will be separation from God and all that is holy and good. John Milton described it in *Paradise Lost:*

A dungeon horrible on all sides round,
As one great furnace, flamed; yet from those flames
No light, but rather darkness visible
Serv'd only to discover sights of woe,
Regions of sorrow, doleful shades, where peace
And rest can never dwell, hope never comes
That comes to all; but torture without end.[2]

Heaven Can Wait?

However glorious heaven may be, all too many Christians don't give it much thought. Philip Yancey wrote, "A strange fact about modern American life: although 71 percent of us believe in an afterlife (says George Gallup), no one much talks about it. Christians believe that we will spend eternity in a splendid place called heaven . . . isn't it a little bizarre that we simply ignore heaven, acting as if it doesn't matter?"[3]

We are seeing more and more articles on old age, death, AIDS, right to die, and out-of-body experiences. But rarely if ever do we read anything about heaven in the magazines or find books on the subject. When we go through a gallery of pre-twentieth century art or look at dusty anthologies of poetry and prose, we discover that heaven was a topic of greater interest in the past. What has happened to us today? Why the general lack of attention to heaven in modern thought and preaching?

If we begin to think of reasons for disinterest in heaven, here are a few conclusions. First of all, in America and most of the Western nations, we live in an affluent society. Most of us have pain relievers to rely upon, enough food, and beautiful surroundings. The biblical promises of those advantages seem to have been dulled for us. We are so caught up with the affairs of this life we give little attention to eternity.

There is another psychological problem. We see people acting fully alive on television who have been dead for years. Well-known personalities like Gary Cooper, Marilyn Monroe, John F. Kennedy, or Martin Luther King appear giving speeches or acting in films as though they were yet alive. People have an idea they *are* still alive. It makes a vast difference in the thinking of young people about death. It may be one of the reasons why the suicide rate among young people has been increasing at an alarming rate.

Throughout our culture we have been led to the idea that we accept death as the end of life on earth. Elisabeth Kübler-Ross, with her five stages of death, has indicated that the "acceptance" stage is the most healthful. The hope of heaven rarely enters into a therapy session. Philip Yancey said, "I have watched in hospital groups as dying patients worked desperately toward a calm stage of acceptance. Strangely, no one ever talked about heaven in those groups; it seemed embarrassing, somehow cowardly. What convulsion of values can have us holding up the prospect of annihilation as brave and that of blissful eternity as cowardly?"[4]

Heaven may seem vague to some of us because our experience is earthbound. How can we conceive of infinity? To imagine an existence which never ends is mind-boggling. Education and the media hinder man from believing anything that cannot be proved in a test tube. At a time when knowledge of the universe is increasing at great speed through the exploration of outer space, the notion of eternity for finite creatures is an absolute mystery. And it will always be a great mystery. Even the apostle Paul did not plumb the depths of it or describe the prospect. He said, "No eye has seen, no ear has heard, no mind has conceived what God has prepared for those who love him" (1 Corinthians 2:9).

Time bound as we are and goal oriented to achievements in our lifetime, we find it strange to anticipate heaven. It sounds boring to the contemporary mind.

What do we do throughout eternity? A person who has worked hard all his life may look forward to retirement, but sometimes relief from responsibility and challenge leads to restlessness.

We live in an age when activity is equated with value and usefulness. "How are you?" "Busy, busy, busy!" When the merry-go-round slows down, will the music of life fade away?

Every day of our lives we are just a breath away from eternity. The believer in Jesus Christ has the promises of heaven. If we believe them, the anticipation of heaven will never be boring. It will be more thrilling than any of the pleasures earth can offer.

Promises of Heaven

On earth we tend to think of ourselves. But in heaven things will be different. We will experience the truth of the catechism, "Man's chief end is to glorify God, and to enjoy him forever." In heaven God, not man, will be at the center of everything. And His glory will be dominant.

Have you ever watched young couples in love communicate without words? Have you been in love yourself? People deeply in love find absolute bliss in each other's presence and wish their moments together would go on forever. If those moments could be frozen, with no sense of passing time, would that be "heaven" for them? Have you ever said, "I wish this moment could last forever"?

I suspect those feelings are a small indication of what it would be like, frozen in time and loving God, enjoying Him, forever. We will never come down from that "mountaintop" experience.

The Bible assures us that heaven is a definite place. Jesus said, "In my Father's house are many rooms; if it were not so, I would have told you. I am going there to prepare a place for you. And if I go and prepare a place for you, I will come back and take you to be with me that you also may be where I am" (John 14:2, 3).

Today homeless people can be found just about everywhere throughout the world. During a recent cold spell many street people suffered, and some died. Those of us who have comfortable homes may want to help those who are less fortunate, but deep inside we may think, "I'm just glad I have a bed tonight, a warm house, and food to eat." If we have never been homeless, it's hard to understand what it would be like.

In some ways, Christians are homeless. Our true home is waiting for us, prepared by the Lord Jesus Christ. "Now we know that if the earthly tent we live in is destroyed, we have a building from God, an eternal house in heaven, not built by human hands. Meanwhile we groan, longing to be clothed with our heavenly dwelling" (2 Corinthians 5:1, 2). If we look at the beauty He has created on earth, can we comprehend what He has furnished for us in heaven?

When people gaze at the Grand Canyon, they are instantly captured by its blazing glory. The earth offers spectacular vistas on every continent, in every country. Many of us have a favorite place which we would describe as "heaven on earth."

It has been my privilege to preach hundreds of sermons in Europe over the years, and a number of times we have preached in Switzerland. My daughter met and married a Swiss psychologist, so we are quite well

224

acquainted with the Alps. Time after time my wife and I have shared the glories and beauties of those mountains—a meadow filled with spring flowers, the *Dent du Midi,* or the Matterhorn. From Geneva we can travel by plane to the south coast of France in thirty minutes. There we see the historic Mediterranean Sea sparkling with diamond-capped waves. We have so many memories of such times together.

But all of these will pale in comparison to what the Designer and Maker of these wonders of nature has prepared for us. Like Abraham, we can be "looking forward to the city with foundations, whose architect and builder is God" (Hebrews 11:10).

Years ago, André Kole, the talented illusionist who traveled all over the world as a representative of a Christian youth organization, wrote about the death of his wife, Aljeana. She had an incurable brain tumor, and for two years she endured incredible suffering. She gradually lost the use of her arms and legs and couldn't move her head or body. She became totally blind. Day after day she could do nothing but lie helplessly in bed. Kole wrote, "While Aljeana was still able to do some speaking, she always shared a poem that ended with these lines: 'We should not long for heaven, if earth held only joy.'"[5]

Heaven is a place, designed by the greatest architect, and it is promised that there we will receive our glorious inheritance.

I don't exactly know what kind of an inheritance I will receive in heaven, but I know it will be magnificent. When we visit someone's home and admire beautiful silver, rugs, or paintings, we might ask, "Is that an heirloom?" The owner might say that it belonged to his mother, and was very valuable to him. My wife, Ruth, has a beautiful chest inlaid with rare pieces of wood which her grandfather built years ago. People are always admiring it and asking where she got it. "I inherited it," she says.

The silver will tarnish, the rugs will be soiled or torn, the chest could burn in a few minutes. The Bible says we will receive "an inheritance that can never perish, spoil or fade—kept in heaven for you" (1 Peter 1:4).

The things that we inherit on earth may be a great blessing or a terrible curse. Countless lives have been ruined by riches left to irresponsible heirs. However, as children of the King, our inheritance will not spoil, nor will it spoil us. What a wonderful promise!

Heaven is the city of our God. He created heaven and He possesses it. "Acknowledge and take to heart this day that the Lord is God in heaven above and on the earth below. There is no other" (Deuteronomy 4:39).

When everything on earth seems to be going wrong, and when we ache to cry out, "God, where are You?" we have the promise that God is in heaven and is in command. It may seem that no one is in charge here, but if that were true, God Himself would be a liar.

God Speaks from Heaven

What is heaven? It's the home that God created and He possesses. His throne room is His headquarters from which He issues His commands, directions, and prophecies. And Jesus sits at His Father's right hand.

I am not sure God talks audibly to us today as He did to Moses on Mt. Sinai—He certainly never has to me. The movies and stage sometimes portray God as an offstage voice, speaking in rolling bass tones, warning the characters or directing their actions. This may make an interesting scenario, but it may be theologically wrong. Moreover, God never directs in a way contrary to His character. When the Scriptures tell us that He will direct our paths, we can be assured that when He is in control, no matter how thorny the path, He will not tell us to jump off a cliff.

How does God speak from heaven? First, He speaks through the Bible, His written Word. This is why I use the phrase "the Bible says." I would not have the authority to say what I do during crusades or in sermons unless it was based upon the Word of God. "All Scripture is God-breathed and is useful for teaching, rebuking, correcting and training in righteousness" (2 Timothy 3:16). The authors of the Old Testament, for example, make it clear that God was speaking to them and through them. More than 3,000 times they said, "Thus saith the Lord," or the equivalent. And that's good enough for me!

God also speaks in nature. When He created the heavens and the earth, He gave us the most incredible, complex, beautiful, orderly universe. He has spoken in such a way that men and women are without excuse if they do not hear and understand the psalmist's praise in saying, "The heavens declare the glory of God; and the firmament showeth his handiwork" (Psalm 19:1 KJV). Because of the clarity of the message, we can also agree with his statement that "The fool says in his heart, 'There is no God'" (Psalm 14:1). As the Bible declares, "For since the creation of the world God's invisible qualities— his eternal power and divine nature—have been clearly seen, being understood from what has been made, so that men are without excuse" (Romans 1:20).

God speaks most clearly and completely through His Son, Jesus Christ, who is revealed for us in the pages of the Bible and is the Word of God incarnate. When God, the Son, stepped out of heaven onto earth in the form of man, He accomplished what God intended Him to do from eternity past. "In the past God spoke to our forefathers through the prophets at many times and in various ways, but in these last days he has spoken to us by his Son, whom he appointed heir of all things, and through whom he made the universe" (Hebrews 1:1, 2).

God also speaks to us through our consciences. This may be a "still, small voice" that will not let us go until we do what we know is right, or it may be a loud, clear indication that God wants us on the path. We might even think of it as a searchlight revealing the way in which we should go, beamed from heaven itself. Proverbs says, "The lamp of the Lord searches the spirit of a man; it searches out his inmost being" (Proverbs 20:27). We must never silence that inner voice—although we must check what we think it is saying against the Scriptures, to be sure that inner voice is not simply our self-will or our emotions.

When God speaks through His Word, we may receive it clearly, or because of our human frailty it may be distorted, something like a scrambled TV signal coming in over the satellite. Sometimes our receivers are tuned. At other times we may have to wait until we can more clearly hear or "receive" the picture.

One family told a harrowing story of being caught in a blinding blizzard while cross-country skiing. Mother, father, and ten-year-old daughter were lost in a stretch of wilderness on the coldest night in January, with a wind chill factor of twenty to forty degrees below zero. They fashioned a little shelter among some fallen trees and developed a plan of survival. Father said, "We're going to pray and sing hymns, and exercise, and eat, and play games. In the morning we'll try to get back up to the ski trails."

The little family knew they faced at least twelve hours of freezing darkness. They began their plan, singing "Onward Christian Soldiers" as they jogged in place. They named all the relatives they could remember, invented stories, made grocery lists, and most important, talked to God. The mother remembered a Bible verse and repeated it so that the little girl and the father could memorize it. "The Lord is near. Do not be anxious about anything, but in everything, by prayer and petition, with thanksgiving, present your requests to God. And the peace of God, which transcends all understanding, will guard your hearts and your minds in Christ Jesus" (Philippians 4:5–7).

As the night wore on, the circumstances worsened. The father recalled later, "I was holding one of the space blankets over the others in a not-very-successful attempt to block out the wind-driven snow, and for the first time I wondered if we were going to make it. But then it was as if God spoke to me and said, 'Don't worry, I'm going to take care of you.'" And He surely did.[6]

God speaks to us from heaven when we pray. Sometimes the answers are clear; sometimes they are vague; sometimes they say "wait." However, we know that someday we will be with Him in His home, and communications will be crystal clear, because we will be with Him. "Now we see but a poor reflection; then we shall see face to face. Now I know in part; then I shall know fully, even as I am fully known" (1 Corinthians 13:12).

What Will *Not* Be in Heaven

In heaven there will be no sectarian worship, no denominational differences, no church creeds. There will be no temple worship, for God and His Son, Jesus Christ, will be the centers of worship (Revelation 21:22).

I was brought up as a Presbyterian and later became a Baptist. But in later years I have felt that I belong to all churches. Ruth has remained a strong Presbyterian, but deep in her heart she, too, belongs to all the other churches. We have never had major differences in our theology despite these backgrounds, but many people do get into heated arguments about denominational doctrines.

God did not invent denominations, man did. When we go to His home, He will invite us in, but will not ask us for our church or Sunday school credentials. Only one question will be asked: "What did you do on earth with My Son, Jesus?" It will make no difference whether we were Catholic or Protestant, Jew or Gentile. What matters is whether we believe in Him or reject Him. Attending a particular church does not guarantee anyone admission to heaven. Corrie ten Boom used to say, "A mouse in a cookie jar isn't a cookie."

In heaven we won't get secondhand knowledge. On earth we listen to pastors, teachers, philosophers, parents, and writers, and sometimes we don't know who to believe. (That secondhand knowledge is important, of course, because God has endowed man with intellect to use and has given the gifts of teaching and preaching to some individuals to help us.)

Some men use their intellect for His glory, others use it for their own. However, in heaven our spiritual intelligence will be perfected by direct contact with the source of all knowledge. If there is a *Daily News of Heaven,* we can be sure we will be able to believe what we read there.

In heaven there will be no fear. We won't need locks on the doors, bars at the windows, or alarm systems. Everything that causes fear will be eliminated. We will walk the golden streets with no concern for danger lurking in doorways. Today, fear stalks the world. We cannot escape it on any corner. Even if we believe we have nothing to fear, our human nature will invent something to fear.

In heaven there will be no night. On earth we equate night with darkness and ignorance; we say, "I was really left in the dark." Light is a symbol of understanding; we may nod our heads as a problem is clarified and say, "Now I see the light!" "The Lord is my light and my salvation—whom shall I fear?" (Psalm 27:1).

Night hides the joyous beauty of the sun, although it has a beauty of its own. But a nightless world will be illumined by His light, making the sun, moon, and stars (and the electric lights of earth) a pale comparison to the authentic masterpiece.

Finally, in heaven there will be no more suffering or death. Think of it! "And I heard a loud voice from the throne saying, 'Now the dwelling of God is with men, and he will live with them. They will be his people, and God himself will be with them and be their God. He will wipe every tear from their eyes. There will be no more death or mourning or crying or pain, for the old order of things has passed away.' He who was seated on the throne said, 'I am making everything new!' Then he said, 'Write this down, for these words are trustworthy and true'" (Revelation 21:3–5).

Homesick for Heaven

When business recruiters visit prospective employees to tell them about their business, they put up a good front. They may woo the recruit with an expensive dinner while they paint a wonderful picture of the company. The description is so exciting that the recruit can hardly wait to begin. However, soon after being hired the new employee discovers that everything isn't quite as rosy as it was originally portrayed.

Will heaven really offer such wonderful benefits that the recruit can't wait to get started?

Vance Havner, who was one of the most quotable pulpiteers of our time, said, "I'm homesick for heaven. It's the hope of dying that has kept me alive this long."[7]

Heaven is a wonderful place and the benefits for the believer are out of this world!

THE OTHER SIDE

This isn't death—it's glory!
It is not dark—it's light!
It isn't stumbling, groping,
Or even faith—it's sight!
This isn't grief—it's having
My last tear wiped away;
It's sunrise—it's the morning
Of my eternal day!

This isn't even praying—
It's speaking face to face;
Listening and glimpsing
The wonders of His grace.
This is the end of pleading

For strength to bear my pain;
Not even pain's dark memory
Will ever live again.

How did I bear the earth-life
Before I knew this rapture
Of meeting face to face
The One who sought me, saved me,
And kept me by His grace![8]

11

BELIEVER'S

DEATH BENEFITS

"Even when we allow our imaginations to run wild on the joys of heaven, we find that our minds are incapable of conceiving what it will be like."

For to me, to live is Christ and to die is gain.

Philippians 1:21

——————————————— —

A little girl was walking with her father in the country. No neon signs, no automobile headlights or street lamps marred the stillness of the crisp evening. As she looked into the deep blue velvet sky, studded with an array of diamonds which put the most dazzling Tiffany display to shame, she said, "Daddy, if the wrong side of heaven is so beautiful, what do you think the right side will be like?"

Some day all believers in Jesus Christ will see the "right side" of heaven.

When will we go to heaven? What will it be like? What will we experience there? I have asked myself those questions and searched the Scriptures for the answers. While we are on earth, I doubt that any of us has his eyes constantly fixed on the glory to come; we have God-given responsibilities to take care of right now. However, knowing the final destination should make our daily life more vigorous, our problems on earth less troublesome.

When the apostle Paul said "to die is gain" he did not mean he wanted to escape his earthly existence. He prefaced it by saying, "For to me, to live is Christ," which is life in its most joyful form, relying upon Christ's love and guidance, strengthened by Him, and loving and being loved by Him. Paul could never be accused by the slur of being "so heavenly minded he was no earthly good."

A Christian's citizenship may be in heaven, but he has obligations as a citizen of earth. Both living with Christ and going to be with Him in death are greatly to be desired.

When Will We Go to Heaven?

The believer's passage to heaven is a direct route. As soon as we are dead, we will be with the Lord. Jesus told the repentant thief on the cross, "I tell you the truth, today you will be with me in paradise" (Luke 23:43). Paul declared, "I desire to depart and be with Christ" (Philippians 1:23). He also affirmed, "Therefore we are always confident and know that as long as we are at home in the body we are away from the Lord. We live by faith, not by sight. We are confident, I say, and would prefer to be away from the body and at home with the Lord" (2 Corinthians 5:6–8).

The moment we take our last breath on earth we take our first in heaven. We are absent from the body and immediately present with the Lord. Then in God's time we receive our glorified bodies at the Second Coming of Christ.

We will be known in our resurrection or heavenly bodies, just as Moses and Elijah were recognized when they appeared with Jesus on the Mount of Transfiguration. Moses had been dead for more than 1,400 years and Elijah had been caught up to heaven in a whirlwind over six centuries before Jesus lived. Here's what happened all those years later: "Jesus took Peter, James, and his brother John to the top of a high and lonely hill, and as they watched, his appearance changed so that his face shone like the sun and his clothing became dazzling white. Suddenly Moses and Elijah appeared and were talking with him. Peter blurted out, 'Sir, it's wonderful that we can be here! If you want me to, I'll make three shelters, one for you and one for Moses and one for Elijah'" (Matthew 17:1–4 LB).

The disciples recognized Moses and Elijah, although they did not yet have their resurrection bodies. This will be explained later. They had recognizable bodies; they were not disembodied, ghostly apparitions.

We will go to heaven immediately, and we will recognize and be recognized. Do some believers have glimpses of loved ones as they approach the gates of heaven? I believe it is possible.

Ruth tells about an experience she had in China. On the station where she lived, one of the evangelistic missionaries was Ad Talbot, whom she affectionately called Uncle Ad. Talbot had five sons and a daughter, Margaret Gay, a girl he deeply loved. Sometime after her death he was in the country with a Chinese Christian woman who was dying. As he knelt beside her bed, the old woman's face lit up and she said to Uncle Ad, "I see heaven, and Jesus is on the right hand of God, and Margaret Gay is with him." At that moment the room was filled with heavenly music and the Chinese woman was dead.

When my grandmother was dying she sat up in her bed, smiled, and said, "I see Jesus, and He has His hand outstretched to me. And there's Ben and he has both of his eyes and both of his legs!" My grandfather had lost a leg and an eye at Gettysburg.

Death has two stages, first the separation of the body from the spirit of a person for a purely spiritual existence, and second, reunion with the body and a glorious resurrection at the Second Coming of Christ.

When our body ceases to function and we are dead, the spirit of the believer is not asleep. Our flesh and bones and all the intricate and wonderful parts God has made are the dwelling place of the spirit of the believer. When we leave our bodies, we depart to be with Christ (Philippians 1:23), and "wait eagerly for our adoption as sons, the redemption of our bodies" (Romans 8:23). Yes, some day our bodies will be renewed and changed, like that of the resurrected body of Jesus Christ.

The story is told of a missionary family who were forced to leave inland China when the enemy took over the country. Each night on their flight to the coast they slept in a different village hut. One night the missionary's wife died quite suddenly and unexpectedly. When morning came he had to explain what had happened to the grief-stricken children.

None of them would consent to leaving their mother's body behind, buried in the soil of a foreign land. If ever the missionary prayed for wisdom and the right words, he did that day as he tried to explain to his children.

He reminded them that they had stayed in a different hut every night, but when morning came and it was time to leave, they continued on their journey, leaving the hut behind. He told the children that their mother's body was the house in which she lived. During the night God told her to come home, so she went, leaving her house behind.

"That house was her body and we loved it," he said, "but Mother no longer lives in it. So we'll leave her here and put her in the ground until the Lord picks her up and takes her body home to be glorified and again restored to her spirit, which is with God now."

That settled the question for them and they left China, certain that their mother had gone on ahead of them to heaven.

If the two stages of death seem difficult to understand, Dr. H. A. Ironside explained them by using this simple illustration which may help. He noticed a shop in his town which was no longer open for business. One day while driving past the building he saw a sign in the window, "Closed for Alterations." The owner had suspended his business dealings with the public long enough to renovate the store. After a time the store was reopened with many changes and improvements. This is a picture of the death of the believer. He moves out of his body until it has been repaired, then, at the resurrection, the inward man will move into his renewed body.

Not Everyone Will Die

Many believers will go to heaven before they die a physical death. The Bible tells us that one generation of believers will never know bodily death. This miraculous and mysterious event is called the "Rapture." We are told that it is a mystery, something that has not been revealed before. Paul says, "Listen, I tell you a mystery: We will not all sleep, but we will all be changed—in a flash, in the twinkling of an eye, at the last trumpet. For the trumpet will sound, the dead will be raised imperishable, and we will be changed" (1 Corinthians 15:51, 52).

What a quick transformation that will be! Scientists tell us that the winking of an eye is the quickest movement of the human body. However, in the Greek, the "twinkling of the eye" implies only half a wink; that was the expression Paul used to describe the change.

What does it mean, that we will be "changed"? Our mortal bodies will become immortal. This means we will be changed in our appearance, but not in our essence. This is why we will recognize people we knew here on earth.

When will these great events take place? Predictions about this happening and the Second Coming are not unique in our time. Today we have people saying, "I believe Jesus will return before the end of this century."

I would not make such predictions, because they are in complete disobedience to the Word of God: "Now, brothers, about times and dates we do not need to write to you, for you know very well that the day of the Lord will come like a thief in the night" (1 Thessalonians 5:1, 2).

Jesus said, "No one knows about that day or hour, not even the angels in heaven, nor the Son, but only the Father" (Matthew 24:36). He also said that we should watch for the signs of the end of the age, and not be caught in the dark. Many Bible believers who have studied the Scriptures and the signs of our times believe that the Rapture may not be far away. Certainly in our lifetime we are seeing an acceleration of those events that Jesus said would be signs of His return.

In recent years I have spoken more and more on the Second Coming of Christ, for this glorious event has been neglected in many of our churches. Also, I cannot help being excited when I see all around me the rapidity with which the announced signs of the end times seem to be happening.

However, I try seriously to avoid two extremes: one is the arrogance of believing I have some special insight about the future and His coming, even if this knowledge seems to be based upon the Bible; the other extreme is to ignore the fact that Christ will return, and for me to live as if His coming were a meaningless myth.

In spite of the wars, the crimes, the agony of many who are living today without freedom, there is the "blessed hope" for all true believers that we could be caught up to meet Christ in the air at any moment (Titus 2:13–15).

The Rapture will take place when Jesus comes for His saints, or all true believers. This will not be seen or understood by the world of unbelievers. Only the Christians will see Him. It will take place quickly and unexpectedly; those who are left will be bewildered as they try to rationalize the sudden disappearance of millions of people.

At the Second Coming, after the Rapture, *everyone* will see Him. His return will be personal and physical. "Look, he is coming with the clouds, and every eye will see him, even those who pierced him; and all the peoples of the earth will mourn because of him" (Revelation 1:7).

The Second Coming of Christ will be sudden. It will be as electrifying as an unexpected flash of lightning. Jesus said, "For as the lightning comes from the east and flashes to the west, so will be the coming of the Son of Man" (Matthew 24:27).

Christ will be accompanied by the believers who have died, returning in immortal, glorified bodies. Who will they be? They will be all of the resurrected saints of the Old Testament and everyone who repented of their sins and received Christ by faith—those who have been saved this side of the Cross.

Many places in the Scriptures tell us of Christ's return accompanied by the "clouds of heaven." The prophet Daniel predicted, "In my vision at night I looked, and there before me was one like a son of man, coming with the clouds of heaven" (Daniel 7:13). In Hebrews 12:1 believers are admonished to serve God righteously because we are constantly surrounded by a "cloud of witnesses." Zechariah says that "the Lord my God will come, and all the holy ones with him" (Zechariah 14:5).

What a thrilling future for those of us who know that some day we will populate the kingdom of God.

Is the Trip Worth It?

Many true Christians disagree on the sequence of events in relation to the Second Coming of Christ. It is not my purpose in this book to propose a theological debate between the premillennial, amillennial, and post-millennial viewpoints. The most important issues are, Will you be in God's kingdom that is now being prepared for us? What will it be like? And how should we live in anticipation of heaven?

I have traveled all over the world and have slept in more hotel and motel rooms, endured more airline flights, and tried to understand more foreign language menus than I care to count. Resorts with year-round swimming pools, and villas with oceanfront views hold some appeal for me, but the older I get the more my idea of a great vacation is to go home, sit on the front porch with Ruth on a spring, summer, or fall evening as the sun is setting, and listen to the katydids and the night noises as they begin; or to sit in an easy chair before a crackling fire in the wintertime with Ruth and gaze out on the mountains.

I had always thought that I would have some years of retirement when I would be able to spend most of my time doing those things. However, to my surprise, God has given me extra strength to preach and write, and to have a ministry at my age that I never dreamed I would have. So I have foregone many of the pleasures of retirement to continue the ministry. This makes heaven an even greater anticipation for me.

God called me many years ago to be an evangelist, and I have never regretted His leading. I love the crusades, meeting people from every country and culture all over the world. My life has been blessed by friends from every land, and challenges from every corner.

However, I cannot help but long so many times in my travels for the serenity of our log house in the mountains of North Carolina.

When we are young and restless to be free, home is the place from which we long to escape. But if there is still a home intact when trouble arises and life becomes a battlefield, home is the place to which we yearn to return. Solomon, who was called the Teacher in Ecclesiastes, expressed this human tendency. He said, "Remember your Creator in the days of your youth, before the days of trouble come and the years approach when you will say, 'I find no pleasure in them'—before the sun and the light and the moon and stars grow dark, and the clouds return after the rain . . ." (Ecclesiastes 12:1, 2).

Solomon tells us when we are stooped with age, when our teeth are gone, when our eyesight and hearing begin to fail, then "man goes to his eternal home and mourners go about the streets" (Ecclesiastes 12:5).

Our temporary homes may be palaces or hovels, but our eternal heavenly home will be bright and beautiful. How could it be any other way? The great Architect and Builder of the universe designed a permanent dwelling place for His children. Earth has its beauty, but man has spoiled so much of it. In heaven there will be no need for environmentalists to work for better air and water quality, or to decry the destruction of our land for housing developments.

When heaven was revealed to the apostle John, he found difficulty describing it, so he used the analogy of a bride, beautifully dressed for her bridegroom. What an apt description. My three daughters are married, and I believe they are all very beautiful, but they were never so radiant and beautiful as on their wedding days!

With five children and eighteen grandchildren, family reunions are difficult to plan. Yet we love being together and hate it when we must part. I have dear friends with whom I enjoy talking for hours. Then we look at the clock, run to keep appointments, and sometimes don't see each other again for years.

In heaven there will be no more sorrowful separations. For many people, life on earth has lost its meaning because a dear one or close friends who were a vital part of life on earth are no longer here. In heaven, we will be together in Christ. We will see the mother or father, the children, brothers, and sisters who have preceded us. We will have a family reunion like no other!

Even when we allow our imaginations to run wild on the joys of heaven, we find that our minds are incapable of conceiving what it will really be like. We are imprisoned by our earthly limitations. Years ago, Rebecca Ruter Springer wrote a little book called *My Dream of Heaven*. One of my friends told me she was given a copy of that book after the death of a loved one and it consoled her by describing the glories of heaven in such a beautiful way that she could appreciate and even anticipate what wonders her loved one was enjoying. The book, in its quaint early nineteenth-century style, was fanciful, but it captured biblical truths with emotional impressions. We wonder, for instance, about some of the things we love on earth. Will we be separated from them in heaven? What about our favorite pets? Is there a place for them? I don't know the exact answers to those questions, but I trust the love of my Lord. Everything needed for our happiness will be there.

In describing her journey *intra muros*, within the gates, Mrs. Springer wrote, "Do you know I think one of the sweetest proofs we have of the Father's loving care for us is, that we so often find in this life the things which gave us great happiness below. The more unexpected this is, the greater joy it brings. I remember once seeing a beautiful little girl enter heaven, the very first to come of a large and affectionate family. I afterward learned that the sorrowful cry of her mother was, 'Oh, if only we had someone there to meet her, to care for her!' She came, lovingly nestled in the Master's own arms, and a little later, as he sat still caressing and talking to her, a remarkably fine Angora kitten, of which the child had been very fond, and which had sickened and died some weeks before, to her great sorrow, came running across the grass and sprang directly in her arms, where it lay contentedly. Such a glad cry as she recognized her little favorite, such hugging and kissing as that kitten received, made joy even in heaven!"[1]

Far-fetched? Why should it be? If to die is gain, as Paul said, then why shouldn't we enjoy even more in heaven the things we loved on earth?

It is often asked, "Will we be married in heaven?" The Sadducees of Jesus' time questioned Him about a woman who had seven husbands. They asked, "At the resurrection whose wife will she be, since the seven were married to her?" Jesus replied, "Are you not in error because you do not know the Scriptures or the power of God? When the dead rise, they will neither marry nor be given in marriage; they will be like the angels in heaven" (Mark 12:23–25).

Someone may object, "But I love my husband (or wife) so much. If we know our loved ones in heaven, why aren't we married?" Also, there are instances in which a person has had more than one marriage, as did the woman to whom the Sadducees referred. The more I meditate on the promises of heaven, the more I have faith that these questions will no longer be relevant, because they will be answered in a glorious manner. I trust Jesus with all my tomorrows, knowing that He will solve the mystery of life beyond the grave.

New Bodies for Old

Scientists have made amazing advances in giving new arms and legs for lost ones, new eyes so the blind can see. Kidney and heart transplants help people extend their life spans. But someday, we shall have complete and perfect new bodies. Today we live in a literal body, but someday "When he comes back he will take these dying bodies of ours and change them into glorious bodies like his own" (Philippians 3:21 LB).

We are guaranteed new bodies because of the resurrection of Jesus Christ from the grave. The central fact of our entire Christian theology is that Jesus rose! No amount of skepticism or alleged "Passover Plots" can blot out the fact that Jesus Christ died on the cross and that in three days He arose from the grave. He appeared to the disciples in His post-resurrection body, walked through the doors they had locked in fear. Thomas, the disciple, was not there, and he said doubtfully, "I'll believe it when I see the nail marks in his hands and in his side." A week later Jesus passed through the locked doors again and said to Thomas, "Put your finger here; see my hands. Reach out your hand and put it into my side. Stop doubting and believe" (John 20:27).

Later Jesus had a fish dinner alongside the Sea of Galilee with His disciples. When He returned in His resurrected body He performed so many miracles, "If every one of them were written down, I suppose that even the whole world would not have room for the books that would be written" (John 21:25).

The resurrection of Jesus Christ guarantees that we will someday have resurrected bodies. He will change or transfigure our bodies, as an ugly caterpillar is changed to a beautiful butterfly. We recognize the magnificent winged creature is the same living being as the fuzzy insect, yet different.

The resurrection is our great hope. In what is called

"the great resurrection chapter" of the Bible, 1 Corinthians 15, Paul wrote, "But if it is preached that Christ has been raised from the dead, how can some of you say that there is no resurrection of the dead? If there is no resurrection of the dead, then not even Christ has been raised. And if Christ has not been raised, our preaching is useless and so is your faith. . . . But Christ has indeed been raised from the dead, the firstfruits of those who have fallen asleep" (1 Corinthians 15:12–14, 20).

The Christians at Corinth did not question that Christ had risen, but they evidently didn't believe others who had died would rise again. However, Paul paints a gloomy picture of what life would be like without belief in the resurrection. He said all preaching would be in vain, faith would be worthless, and all Christian belief would be false.

Kenneth Chafin wrote in his commentary on the epistles to the Corinthians, "I remember hearing a person say once that even if Christ had not been raised from the dead, he thought he would continue to live the Christian life because 'it would still be the best way to live.' But I wonder if he didn't say that because he could not conceive what it would be like to live in a world without the hope of the resurrection."[2]

A Superhuman Body

What kind of a body will a resurrected believer have? It's difficult for us to imagine what someone would be like with any other than a physical body. We can visualize a different earthly body, and many people do this. Some women put pictures of movie stars or models on the refrigerator door to remind themselves of the body they would like to have. Men imagine themselves as an athlete, or perhaps as Rocky, invincible in their physical abilities. But there are very few in the entire world who have what might be called "ideal bodies." And yet, some day, we will have them. Paul has given us a pretty good description of what those bodies will be like.

First, the resurrection body is compared to a seed planted in the ground which produces a plant or a flower. Anyone who has ever gardened knows how miraculous it is to see a towering tomato plant, with yellow blossoms that become huge tomatoes, grow from a tiny seed. The seed and the plant are the continuous life of a single entity, just as our physical body, planted in death, will have the same individuality as our resurrection body. We will be recognized as ourselves, not some genetic version without a distinctive label.

"It is sown in dishonor, it is raised in glory; it is sown in weakness, it is raised in power" (1 Corinthians 15:43). The body that lies in the grave has been neglected. It may be worn out with age, abused by disease, or broken by an accident, but in the resurrection that body is raised in glory! It will be free of all infirmities. Joni Eareckson Tada will throw away her wheelchair. Dr. Bob Pierce will be free of cancer. Helen Keller will see and hear and speak. Those who were burned or maimed in wars will be whole. Old people will be young and vigorous.

In our resurrection bodies we will know nothing of physical weakness. Limitations imposed on us on this earth are not known in heaven. We will have a habitation from God that is incorruptible, immortal, and powerful.

"Yes, they are weak, dying bodies now, but when we live again they will be full of strength. They are just human bodies at death, but when they come back to life they will be superhuman bodies" (1 Corinthians 15:43, 44 LB).

That verse makes me chuckle when I see myself today and think that someday I'll be like Superman, without the red cape and tights. However, in spite of this exciting prospect, I want to keep this present body in as good shape as I can for the work that the Lord has for me to do while I'm still on earth.

"For our earthly bodies, the ones we have now that can die, must be transformed into heavenly bodies that cannot perish but will live forever. When this happens, then at last this Scripture will come true—'Death is swallowed up in victory.' O death, where then your victory? Where then your sting? For sin—the sting that causes death—will all be gone; and the law, which reveals our sins, will no longer be our judge. How we thank God for all of this! It is he who makes us victorious through Jesus Christ our Lord!

"So, my dear brothers, since future victory is sure, be strong and steady, always abounding in the Lord's work, for you know that nothing you do for the Lord is ever wasted as it would be if there were no resurrection" (1 Corinthians 15:53–58 LB).

What a promise! Christ lives. We shall live. He has a glorious, resurrected body, and so shall we! This is how a Christian can live and die with hope. Death is swallowed up in victory.

Beyond the Body Beautiful

There is more to a Christian's death benefits than a fine body. Some people place so much emphasis upon the care and feeding of this temporary shelter that the over whelming problems of a sick world get little or no attention. We do not have a paradise on earth, it is riddled with so much sin and disease.

The first great benefit of death for Christians is permanent freedom from evil. When Paul talked about his desire to "depart and to be with Christ" (Philippians 1:23), he was conveying the idea of leaving something permanently behind. Everything that is not useful is left—all of the pain, the care, and the anguish of the world. Crime, drugs, war, hatred, starvation, all of the horrors of man's inhumanity to man will be cancelled out of our heavenly existence.

When John was given the Revelation and had caught a glimpse of the Holy City, the New Jerusalem, he said, "There shall be nothing in the city which is evil" (Revelation 22:3 LB).

Freedom! Men have searched for it and died for it, but they will never attain it unless they know Jesus Christ. The message of the old cowboy song, "Don't Fence Me In," will be an eternal reality.

The second benefit of death to believers is that we will be like Jesus. John writes, "Dear friends, now we are children of God, and what we will be has not yet been made known. But we know that when he appears we shall be like him, for we shall see him as he is" (1 John 3:2).

Our imaginations are so stilted. The very thought of being like Jesus is breathtaking. We will be like Him in righteousness. Our old sin nature will be forgotten, erased from our memories forever.

We shall be like Him in knowledge. We have the Holy Spirit to guide us in our understanding of the Word of God here on earth, but our "understanding" is always limited and mixed with error. We struggle to understand the Scriptures, but sometimes even great Bible scholars differ over the exact interpretation of certain passages.

However, everything that puzzled us in life will be made clear. All our "whys" will be answered.

Do you have many unanswered questions today? Our IQs in heaven will far surpass those of the most brilliant people on earth.

We will also be like Jesus in love. Today we are so centered on self, but our death policy says that we will be heirs to the selfless, self-sacrificing love of Jesus Christ. We may find it difficult to love everyone on earth, but in heaven love will be freely given and freely received.

So the supreme benefit, the one which surpasses all others, is that we will be with Jesus Christ. I long to see Him face to face, to hear His voice and touch Him. In the day I go to be with Him, there will be no unfulfilled longings or disappointments. He will welcome me into His mansion, answer my questions, and teach me the wisdom of the ages.

Once we meet Him, what will happen? Will He be glad to see us?

I must ask myself, "Billy Graham, are you prepared to meet the Master at any moment?" Yes, I am—but not because I have preached or tried to help people, but solely because I am trusting Christ as my Lord and Savior.

Stop right now and ask yourself that question.

12

BEFORE

I DIE

"When we build a house we lay the foundation first. After that we choose the material for the walls, floors, and roof. The believer has his foundation in Jesus Christ. Now we are to build upon this foundation, and the work we have done must stand the ultimate test . . . ."

For we must all appear before the judgment seat of Christ, that each one may receive what is due him for the things done while in the body, whether good or bad.

2 Corinthians 5:10

In the last days before a Christian goes to be with the Lord, Satan will seek to steal his peace. The weakness caused by disease or pain, the confusion of the mind, may cause even the greatest saints to have moments of doubt.

Before one of America's greatest theologians and Bible teachers died, he called me frequently seeking assurance of his eternal salvation. At first I didn't understand how this man of God, a teacher of the Word, could be troubled with questions about his worthiness. However, I have discovered this problem is not uncommon, and loved ones should be available to offer help and hope without provoking a sense of guilt.

Few women in our generation have had greater influence upon the world than Corrie ten Boom. Her biographer wrote, "A Christian witness meets its true test in times of suffering. Pastor Chuck Mylander visited her often after her first crippling stroke, and only once did he see her upset about her own needs. As is very common in stroke patients, a wave of doubt about the Lord's nearness had swept over her. Pam Rosewell explained what Corrie couldn't fully communicate, and as he questioned Corrie, tears coursed across her wrinkled cheeks.

"Pastor Mylander took out his Bible and read from Matthew 28, where Jesus said, 'Lo, I am with you always, even to the end of the age.' He reminded Corrie that this promise was for those who gave themselves to fulfill the Great Commission, as she had done so faithfully. Her face brightened as she began to speak with confidence, 'Always, always, always.'"[1]

When the final moments come, the power of God will conquer and the believer will enjoy the comfort of His loving arms.

Signs for a Peaceful Exit

Herbert Lockyer tells about finding an ancient work called *The Book of the Craft of Dying.* The unknown writer of this early treatise discussed five principal temptations confronting the believer. Translating them into modern vernacular, they are worthy of examination.

1. *Faith must be maintained.* This is what so many seek, when doubt clouds the mind as the last hour approaches. It does not seem to matter how long the Christian has walked in the path of faith. As with Corrie, the questioning sometimes comes. We are all like children who constantly need to be told that we are loved.

2. *Desperation must be avoided.* Another wile of the

devil is to bring up past sins and parade them before the mind of the Christian. We have been forgiven, and there is no need to pull out the past and review it morbidly. "Everyone who believes in him receives forgiveness of sins through his name" (Acts 10:43).

3. *Impatience must be avoided.* When we come to die of old age or disease or accident, we should await the final outcome patiently. Dr. Bob Pierce who was the founder of World Vision and Samaritan's Purse, the ministry my son, Franklin, has continued, was in the last hours of his life, suffering from leukemia. In his final letter he wrote, "Now I am living totally in 'God Room.' No known human skill can further prolong my life and I am gloriously living and working in that space reaching beyond the utmost man and science can do. This is the area where miracles begin. If the greatest human skills and genius can do it, God is not required and it is no miracle. Miracles only begin at the point just beyond all furthest stretch of human ingenuity and possibility of accomplishment. That is God Room!"

Dr. Bob was patient, but hopeful, to the end.

4. *Complacence must not rule.* When Satan can't shake the faith of a believer, nor cause him to despair or be impatient, he may tempt him through spiritual pride. "Look how many good deeds I have done, how great my service has been for the Lord," may be the boast. We are taught in the Scriptures that we are saved by grace, through faith, it is a gift of God, so that no one can boast (Ephesians 2:9).

5. *The temporal must not dominate.* I can understand this more than any other. We are all so possessed by our possessions and absorbed in our earthly obligations that we set our minds on temporal and impermanent things, rather than fully committing ourselves to God.[2]

259

We may not encounter any of these temptations, but if we do we must remember that the Bible says, "No temptation has overtaken you but such as is common to man; and God is faithful, who will not allow you to be tempted beyond what you are able; but with the temptation will provide the way of escape also, that you may be able to endure it" (1 Corinthians 10:13 NASB).

Last Words of Saints

An old hymn says,

> Teach me to live that I may dread
> The grave as little as my bed;
> Teach me to die, that so I may
> Rise glorious at the Judgment Day.

Many times the dying words of believers have been recorded by family members and biographers. These expressions of faith and trust illustrate the mighty power of God at a time when human resources have been drained.

In the sixteenth century there was a bloody purge of Christians in Scotland who died for their faith. Thousands of ministers and laymen suffered for Christ's sake. Many were hanged on the gibbet or slaughtered in cold blood. Some of these believers endured the torture of burning at the stake or being beheaded. The last words of these heroes and martyrs prove the truth of Christ's promise He made to His disciples. He warned them, "I am sending you out as sheep among wolves . . . . Yes, and you must stand trial before governors and kings for my sake. This will give you the opportunity to tell them about me, yes, to witness to the world" (Matthew 10:16–18 LB).

In their final hour of agony, men and women who have suffered and died for His sake are given the words to say and the courage to die.

Patrick Hamilton was a young Scotsman, twenty-four years old, when he was condemned and sentenced to die. As he was hurried to the stake and the fire was burning he pulled off his outer garments and handed them to his servant, saying, "These will not profit me in the fire, yet they will do thee some good." Hamilton was taunted by one of his persecutors to deny God, but answered, "Wicked man! Thou knowest I am not at guilt, and that it is the truth of God for which I now suffer."

As the fire burned, the young martyr called out, "How long, O Lord, shall darkness overwhelm this realm? How long wilt Thou suffer this tyranny of man?" As he was being consumed by the flames he prayed like the biblical Stephen, "Lord Jesus, receive my spirit."[3]

Donald Cargill was a bright star in the history of Scottish persecutions. He was condemned by the government as "one of the most seditious preachers and a villainous and fanatical conspirator," and sentenced to the gallows. When he came to the scaffold, Cargill said these moving words, although it was said that the drums were beaten in an attempt to drown out his voice·

Now I am near to getting to my crown, which shall be sure; for I bless the Lord, and desire all of you to bless Him that He hath brought me here, and makes me triumph over devils, and men, and sin . . . they shall wound me no more. I forgive all men the wrongs they have done to me, and pray the Lord may forgive all the wrongs that any of the elect have done against Him. I pray that sufferers may be kept from sin, and helped to know their duty . . . farewell reading and preaching, praying and believing, wanderings, reproaches, and sufferings. Welcome joy unspeakable and full of glory.[4]

As Martin Luther was dying he repeated three times, "Into Thy hands I commend my spirit! Thou hast redeemed me, O God of Truth."

John Milton's farewell was, "Death is the great key that opens the palace of Eternity."

Lew Wallace, the author of *Ben Hur*, had a sentence from the Lord's Prayer on his lips, "Thy will be done."

In his last will and testament Shakespeare said, "I commend my soul into the hands of God my Creator, hoping and assuredly believing, through the merits of Jesus Christ my Savior, to be made partaker of life everlasting; and my body to the earth, whereof it is made."

Michelangelo's last words to those at his bedside were, "Through life remember the sufferings of Jesus."[5]

I do not know whether we will suffer for the cause of Christ. But throughout the world today there are people who are enduring cruelties and persecution because of their Christian faith. We must pray for them, and for ourselves, so that in our own dying hour God will give us grace to endure until the end, anticipating the certainty of His glory to come.

We Are Accountable

Before we die two basic issues must be resolved. The first is, "Am I ready?" Have you confessed your sins and asked Jesus Christ to come into your heart, to take possession of your life? Millions of Christians throughout the world are assured "That if you confess with your mouth, 'Jesus is Lord,' and believe in your heart that God raised him from the dead, you will be saved" (Romans 10:9).

But the Christian life doesn't end there! The next basic issue is "How then do I live?" This is to say, before you die, what service will you render to God and man? Are you investing your life in those things that will last for eternity? "So we make it our goal to please him, whether we are at home in the body or away from it. For we must all appear before the judgment seat of Christ, that each one may receive what is due him for the things done while in the body, whether good or bad" (2 Corinthians 5:9–10).

The Bible says we will all have to give account to Jesus someday (1 Peter 4:5). We will stand before the Judgment Seat of Christ (Romans 14:10). On that day, what we have done on earth will be past. Our chances to speak to the neighbor about the love of Christ, to give to missions, to help evangelism, will be over. Opportunities to share our earthly goods with the starving will be gone. Whatever gifts we were given will be worthless if we hoarded them on earth.

The Ultimate Test

When we build a house we lay the foundation first. After that we choose the material for the walls, floors, and roof. Some buildings are put up for planned obsolescence. From a distance they may look slick and modern, but they cannot stand the test of time.

The believer has his foundation in Jesus Christ. Now we are to build upon this foundation, and the work we have done must stand the ultimate test; final exams come at the Judgment Seat of Christ when we receive our rewards.

Paul explained this building process when he said:

> No one can ever lay any other real foundation than that one we already have—Jesus Christ. But there are various kinds of materials that can be used to build on that foundation. Some use gold and silver and jewels; and some build with sticks, and hay, or even straw! There is going to come a time of testing at Christ's Judgment Day to see what kind of material each builder has used. Everyone's work will be put through the fire so that all can see whether or not it keeps its value, and what was really accomplished. Then every workman who has built on the foundation with the right materials, and whose work still stands, will get his pay. But if the house he has built burns up, he will have a great loss. He himself will be saved, but like a man escaping through a wall of flames (1 Corinthians 3:11–15 LB).

We will be judged according to the secret motives and the character of our work. If we have done our work for selfish motives or personal gain, even if the results looked noble to our friends and family, God knows our hearts.

Also, we will be judged according to our ability. Some Christians are capable of more than others, physically, financially, or intellectually. The grandmother living on a small pension but faithfully teaching her little grandchild Bible verses will not be judged for her giving a pittance to missions in the same manner as the business couple with a double income, living in a house beyond their means. The retired couple who count the offering every Sunday, never divulging the amount anyone in the congregation contributes, will not be tested in the same way as the millionaire who wants an inscription on the stained glass window, so everyone will know who donated it.

Some of the most severe tests will be given to the pastors and teachers for the way in which they handled the Word of God. There will be no reward for leading others astray in lifestyle or in doctrine through false teaching.

The Judgment Seat of Christ is referred to as the Greek word *bema,* which identifies the judge's seat in the arena of the Olympic games. The *bema* was the seat where the judge sat, not to punish contestants, but to present awards to the victors. When Christians stand before the *bema* of Christ, it is for the purpose of being rewarded according to their works.

When Christ returns, every Christian will stand before the *bema,* not as spectators, but as those to be judged. The Bible doesn't say where this judgment will take place, and the logistics of millions of saints standing there are beyond comprehension. But one thing is certain, we must all appear.

The Judgment Seat of Christ will be graduation ceremonies at which time each believer will receive a reward for his works. The New Testament teaches these rewards are called "crowns."

We will surely be surprised to note who receives the crowns and who doesn't. The lowliest servant may sparkle with more jewels than the philanthropist who endowed the church and whose name is engraved on the plaque in the narthex.

We all long for appreciation, which doesn't always come from those around us; however, we have assurance that Jesus knows the intentions of our hearts and what we do in secret. "Therefore, my dear brothers, stand firm.

Let nothing move you. Always give yourselves fully to the work of the Lord, because you know that your labor in the Lord is not in vain" (1 Corinthians 15:58).

Five Minutes after I'm in Heaven

My wife saved an article from *Moody Monthly,* pub lished over thirty years ago. When she gave it to me, 1 was working on this book and I marveled how the Lord brings information to us just at the right moment.

At the beginning of the book I quoted my father-in-law's comment, "Only those who are prepared to die are really prepared to live." I want to know how to live so that I may learn how to die. Final exams may, in fact, be tomorrow.

FIVE MINUTES AFTER . .

It may be a moment, or after months of waiting, but soon I shall stand before my Lord. Then in an instant all things will appear in new perspective.

Suddenly the things I thought important—tomorrow's tasks, the plans for the dinner at my church, my success or failure in pleasing those around me—these will matter not at all. And the things to which I gave but little thought—the word about Christ to the man next door, the moment (how short it was) of earnest prayer for the Lord's work in far-off lands, the confessing and forsaking of that secret sin—will stand as real and enduring.

Five minutes after I'm in heaven I'll be overwhelmed by the truths I've known but somehow never grasped. I'll realize then that it's what I am in Christ that comes first with God, and that when I am right with Him, I do the things which please Him.

I'll sense that it was not just how much I gave that mattered, but how I gave—and how much I withheld.

In heaven I'll wish with all my heart that I could reclaim a thousandth part of the time I've let slip through my fingers, that I could call back those countless conversations which could have glorified my Lord—but didn't.

Five minutes after I'm in heaven, I believe I'll wish with all my heart that I had risen more faithfully to read the Word of God and wait on Him in prayer—that I might have known Him while still on earth as He wanted me to know Him.

A thousand thoughts will press upon me, and though overwhelmed by the grace which admits me to my heavenly home, I'll wonder at my aimless earthly life. I'll wish . . . if one may wish in heaven—but it will be too late.

Heaven is real and hell is real, and eternity is but a breath away. Soon we shall be in the presence of the Lord we claim to serve. Why should we live as though salvation were a dream—as though we did not know?

"To him that knoweth to do good, and doeth it not, to him it is sin."

There may yet be a little time. A new year dawns before us. God help us to live now in the light of a real tomorrow![6]

Looking Homeward

I'm not afraid to die, for I know the joys of heaven are waiting. My greatest desire is to live today in anticipation of tomorrow and be ready to be welcomed into His home for all eternity. Will you be making the journey with me?

A Closing Word

"There is no more urgent and critical question in life than that of your personal relationship with God and your eternal salvation."

Throughout this book we have faced honestly the reality of death and how we should deal with it. We have seen also the wonderful promises of God concerning eternal life, and the glory that awaits every believer on the other side of death in heaven.

Perhaps, however, as you have read this book you have had to face the fact that you are not ready to die. You do not know for sure that you will go to heaven when you die, and you have no assurance that God is with you right now as you face illness and suffering. You have never experienced the peace and security that come from a personal relationship with Him.

There is no more urgent and critical question in life than that of your personal relationship with God and your eternal salvation. But can you know—really know—that you will go to heaven when you die? Yes, you can know, and I invite you to make that discovery today.

What must you do? First, you must acknowledge that you are a sinner and repent of your sins. As we have seen in this book, there is only one thing that will keep you out of heaven, and that is your sin. The Bible says, "For all have sinned and fall short of the glory of God" (Romans 3:23). God is pure and holy, and we have no right to enter His presence because we are sinners. No matter how good we are, we can never be good enough to go to heaven on our own merit because His standard is perfection. We need to repent—to turn from our sins.

Second, you must trust Christ alone for your salvation. Christ did for us what we could never do for ourselves. He was without sin—but He took upon Himself your sin and mine when He died on the cross. We deserved only the judgment of God, but Christ willingly suffered the judgment and death we deserved. He died in your place, because He loves you. And now God offers you forgiveness and salvation as a free gift. "For the wages of sin is death, but the gift of God is eternal life in Christ Jesus our Lord" (Romans 6:23).

How do you receive Christ personally and make your decision to follow Him? The Bible says, "Yet to all who received him, to those who believed in his name, he gave the right to become children of God" (John 1:12). Notice in that verse that we are to "believe" and to "receive" Christ. We are to *believe* that He died on the cross for us and rose again from the dead so we could be saved, and we are to *receive* Him personally into our hearts. God has done everything that is necessary to make our salvation possible—but (like any other gift) we must receive it.

Right now I invite you to pray a prayer we have seen people all over the world pray, asking Christ to forgive them and inviting Him to come into their hearts as their Lord and Savior. Will you sincerely pray this prayer now?

"O God, I know that I am a sinner and need Your forgiveness. I believe that You died for my sins. I want to turn from my sins. I now invite You to come into my heart and life. I want to trust You as Savior and follow You as Lord, in the fellowship of Your church. In Christ's name, Amen."

If you have asked Christ into your heart and committed your life to Him, then God has forgiven you and adopted you into His family. More than that, He has promised to save you and bring you into His heavenly kingdom forever—and God cannot lie. "God has given us eternal life, and this life is in his Son. He who has the Son has life; he who does not have the Son of God does not have life. I write these things to you who believe in the name of the Son of God so that you may know that you have eternal life" (1 John 5:11–13).

May God bless you as you commit your life to Christ and follow Him every day. And as you face that day in the future when God will call you to be with Him forever in heaven, may you say with the apostle Paul, "I know whom I have believed, and am convinced that he is able to guard what I have entrusted to him for that day" (2 Timothy 1:12).

Billy Graham

Endnotes

Chapter 1

1. *Time* Magazine, Sept. 22, 1986.
2. Mencken, H. L., *A New Dictionary of Quotations* (New York: Alfred A. Knopf, 1966) 260.

Chapter 2

1. Aries, Phillippe, *Western Attitudes toward Death: From the Middle Ages to the Present* (Baltimore and London: Johns Hopkins University Press, 1974) 9.
2. Ibid., 13.
3. Aries, Phillippe, *The Hour of Our Death* (New York: Alfred A. Knopf, 1981).
4. Ibid.
5. Gallup, George, Jr., with William Proctor, *Adventures in Immortality* (New York: McGraw-Hill, 1982) 185–190.
6. Ibid., 75.
7. MacArthur, Jack, *Exploring in the Next World* (Minneapolis, Minn.: Dimension Books, 1967) 91.
8. Mencken, H. L., *A New Dictionary of Quotations* (New York: Alfred A. Knopf, 1966) 548.
9. Dempsey, David, *The Way We Die* (New York: McGraw-Hill, 1977) 17.
10. Bane, J. Donald, Kutscher, Austin H., Neal, Robert E. and Reeves, Robert, Jr., Editors, *Death and Ministry* (New York: Seabury Press, 1975) 151.
11. Ibid., 150.

Chapter 3

1. Dempsey, David, *The Way We Die* (New York: McGraw-Hill, 1977) 67.
2. Ibid., 53.
3. Ibid., 76.
4. *Los Angeles Times*, Sept. 29, 1986.

Chapter 4

1. American Tract Society, Box 191, Lake Grove, L.I. 1110.
2. Bayly, Joseph, "When a Child Dies," *Family Life Today*, March, 1976.
3. Rogers, Dale Evans, *Angel Unaware* (Old Tappan, N.J.: Spire Books, Fleming H. Revell, 1963) 9.
4. *Los Angeles Times*, Feb. 3, 1986, Part IV.
5. Marshall, Eric, and Hample, Stuart, *Children's Letters to God* (New York: Simon & Schuster, 1966).
6. Krementz, Jill, *How It Feels When a Parent Dies* (New York: Alfred A. Knopf, 1981).
7. Simpson, Michael A., *The Facts of Death* (Englewood Cliffs, N. J.: Prentice-Hall, Inc., 1979) 184.
8. Lewis, C. S., *The Problem of Pain* (New York: Macmillan Publishing, 1962) 93.

Chapter 5

1. Lockyer, Herbert, *Last Words of Saints and Sinners* (Grand Rapids: Kregel Publications, 1969) 65.
2. *Reader's Digest*, Nov., 1986, p. 203.
3. Kopp, Ruth, *When Someone You Love Is Dying* (Grand Rapids: Zondervan, 1980) 20.
4. Ibid., 44.

5. Lockyer, Herbert, *All the Promises of the Bible* (Grand Rapids: Zondervan, 1962) 200.
6. Barfield, Velma, *Woman on Death Row* (Nashville: Oliver-Nelson Books, 1985) 141.
7. Kübler-Ross, Elisabeth, *Therapeutic Grand Rounds*, Number 36, July 10, 1972.

Chapter 6

1. *Time*, Oct. 6, 1986, p. 35.
2. Bioethics Committee Report, Sept. 25, 1986.
3. NCCB Committee for Pro-Life Activities, June 1986.
4. Ibid.
5. *Christian Medical Society Journal*, Summer 1986, p. 17.
6. *Santa Monica Evening Outlook*, May 14, 1986.
7. Barnard, Dr. Christiaan, *Good Life, Good Death* (Englewood Cliffs, N.J.: Prentice-Hall, Inc., 1981) 15.
8. Barnard, op. cit., 66.
9. Alexander, L., "Medical Science Under Dictatorship," *New England Journal of Medicine*, 1949;241:39–47.
10. "The Physician's Responsibility toward Hopelessly Ill Patients." *New England Journal of Medicine*, 1984; 310:955–959.
11. *Newsweek*, Feb. 7, 1983, p. 13.
12. *Time*, July 7, 1980.
13. Sherrill, John, *Mother's Song* (Lincoln, Va.: Chosen Books, 1982) 132, 133, 144.
14. Graham, Ruth Bell, *Sitting by My Laughing Fire* (Waco, Tex.: Word Books, 1977) 178.

Chapter 7

1. Schaeffer, Edith, *Christianity Today*, Mar. 6, 1987, p. 20.

2. Shneidman, Edwin, *Voices of Death* (New York: Harper and Row, 1980) 138.
3. Ibid., 135.
4. Ibid., 137.
5. Tournier, Paul, *The Adventure of Living* (New York. Harper and Row, 1965) 104, 105.
6. *Christianity Today,* Mar. 6, 1987, p. 185
7. Will, George, *Newsweek,* Jan. 9, 1978.
8. Ibid.
9. Tournier, op. cit., 104.
10. Richards, Larry/Johnson, Paul, M.D., *Death and the Caring Community* (Portland, Ore.: Multnomah Press, 1980) 158.

Chapter 8

1. Vanauken, Sheldon, *A Severe Mercy* (New York: Harper and Row, 1980) 180.
2. Westberg, Granger, *Good Grief* (Philadelphia: Fortress Press, 1962) 324.
3. Manning, Doug, *Comforting Those Who Grieve* (New York: Harper and Row, 1985) 71.
4. Graham, Morrow, *They Call Me Mother Graham* (Old Tappan, N.J.: Fleming H. Revell, 1977) 28.
5. Ibid., 31.
6. Ibid.

Chapter 9

1. Pollock, John, *Billy Graham* (Grand Rapids: Zondervan Publishing Co., 1966) 173.
2. Bulletin of Wheaton College, Nov., 1966.

3. Pollock, John, *Billy Graham* (New York: Harper and Row, 1979, Special Crusade Edition) 170–171.
4. Radio message by Dr. James T. Jeremiah, Cedarville College, Dec. 11, 1972.
5. Sanderson, Jim, *Los Angeles Times*, Mar. 5, 1986.
6. Lockyer, Herbert, *Last Words of Saints and Sinners* (Grand Rapids: Kregel Publications, 1969) 114.

Chapter 10

1. Encyclopedia Americana, Vol. 14 (Danbury, Conn.: Grolier, Inc., 1986) 68.
2. Mencken, H. L., *A New Dictionary of Quotations* (New York. Alfred A. Knopf, 1966) 527.
3. Yancey, Philip, "Heaven Can't Wait," *Christianity Today,* Sept. 7, 1984.
4. Ibid.
5. Kole, André, "To Be Continued," *Worldwide Challenge,* April, 1977, p. 27.
6. *Guideposts,* February 1987, p. 27.
7. *Christianity Today,* Nov. 7, 1986.
8. Nicholson, Martha Snell, *Christian Medical Society Journal,* Vol. X, Number 1, Winter, 1979.

Chapter 11

1. Springer, Rebecca Ruter, *My Dream of Heaven* (Forest Grove, Ore.: Book Searchers) 42.
2. *The Communicator's Commentary,* Vol. 7 (Waco, Tex.: Word Books, 1985) 184.

Chapter 12

1. Carlson, Carole, *Corrie, Her Life and Her Faith* (Old Tappan, N.J.: Fleming H. Revell, 1983) 217.
2. Lockyer, Herbert, *Last Words of Saints and Sinners* (Grand Rapids: Kregel Publications, 1969) 220, 221.
3. Ibid., 185.
4. Ibid., 196.
5. Ibid., 73, 105, 109, 110, 125.
6. *Moody Monthly,* January, 1952.